WORKING WITH DIFFERENCES IN COMMUNITIES

A handbook for those who care
about creating inclusive communities

Ann C. Schauber

Illustrated by Rebecca Kirk

OREGON STATE UNIVERSITY EXTENSION SERVICE

Manual 13
March 2002

Oregon State University Extension Service, Corvallis, OR

© 2002 Oregon State University
Published 2002
Printed in the United States of America

This publication was produced and distributed in furtherance
of the Acts of Congress of May 8 and June 30, 1914.
Extension work is a cooperative program of Oregon State
University, the U.S. Department of Agriculture, and Oregon
counties.

Oregon State University Extension Service offers educational programs, activities, and materials—*without
discrimination based on race, color, religion, sex, sexual
orientation, national origin, age, marital status, disability, or
disabled veteran or Vietnam-era veteran status*. Oregon State
University Extension Service is an Equal Opportunity
Employer.

Extension & Station Communications
Oregon State University
422 Kerr Administration
Corvallis, OR 97333
Fax: 541-737-0817
E-mail: puborders@orst.edu
Web: http://eesc.orst.edu

ISBN 1-931979-01-4

**OREGON STATE
UNIVERSITY**

EXTENSION SERVICE

CONTENTS

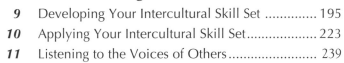

PREFACE

Through my intercultural communication workshops with Extension and other community groups over the past 10 years, I have encountered hundreds of people who want to make their communities, workplaces, and organizations more welcoming to everyone. This book is written in the belief that by working on our own personal intercultural development, we can create more inclusive communities.

Drawing on my knowledge and experience in intercultural communication, my goal is to focus on what "I," the individual, can do to make communities work for everyone. I want to change the focus from what others need to do to what each of us can do to create change.

Since the fundamental message here is that "I" am the one who must learn and adapt (not "them"), this book might be difficult to work with at times. The pages where you feel the most resistance might be those that hold the most potential for learning.

For me, learning to understand and adapt to cultural differences is the most difficult work I have ever done. It also is the richest and most rewarding. When I apply the mind–heart–skill sets outlined in this book, new possibilities emerge for living and working with those who are very different from me. It takes time to process and practice what is written here. Be patient with yourself.

I recognize that this book is written from my own cultural frame of reference. Someone who comes from a different cultural worldview might describe a different approach. I see that possibility as a complement to what I have written.

My wish for you is to have a grand adventure in learning through this book. May you develop deep, rich relationships with others and become a part of new solutions to your communities' problems.

Ann C. Schauber
McMinnville, Oregon
March 2002

ACKNOWLEDGMENTS

I would like to acknowledge my teacher, Dr. Stella Ting-Toomey, University of California, Fullerton, for her guidance, insight, and modeling of what it means to be an effective intercultural communicator.

I also want to acknowledge the directors (Drs. Janet and Milton Bennett), faculty, staff, and students at the Summer Institute for Intercultural Communication. Over the past 10 years, they have provided a multicultural learning laboratory where I can make mistakes and learn from them.

I want to thank the Union Institute faculty and learners who guided me through my doctoral journey in intercultural communication and organizational change. They have strengthened my belief in the possibility of creating inclusive communities.

Thanks to the OSU Extension Service for its commitment to diversity work. I am most grateful to my editors, Teresa Welch and Alan Kirk, who have supported me in this effort not only through their careful editing for clear meaning but also with their enthusiasm for this project. Teresa honored the vision for this book through her artistic layout of the text and art.

Ellen Summerfield, June Harper, Pamala Morris, Michael Keller, and Lori McGraw reviewed drafts of this book. Thank you for adding clarity to my words.

I am indebted to the artist, Rebecca Kirk, for capturing so magically the heart of the meaning in this book.

Thanks to my family, who understood when I was not present with them because I was deep inside this book. Finally, I give my deepest acknowledgment to Alan, the one who holds my hand as we walk through life together.

The publishers have generously given permission to use extended quotations or illustrations from the following copyrighted works: *About Learning,* by Bernice McCarthy, copyright 1996, reprinted by permission of About Learning, Inc., Barrington, IL. *All God's Children Need Traveling Shoes,* copyright 1997, reprinted by Permission of Random House, Inc., New York. *Always Running: La Vida Loca, Gang Days in L.A.,* by Luis Rodriguez, copyright 1994, reprinted by permission of Curbstone Press, Willimantic, CT. *Black Rage,* by William H. Grier and Price M. Cobbs, copyright 1968, reprinted by permission of Perseus Books Group, New York, NY. *Communicating Across Cultures,* by Stella Ting-Toomey, copyright 1999, reprinted by permission of Guilford Press, New York, NY. *The Dance of Life: The Other Dimension of Time,* by Edward T. Hall, copyright 1983, reprinted by permission of Doubleday, a division of Random House, Inc., New York, NY. "Do You Know Why They All Talk at Once? Thoughts on Cultural Differences Between Hispanics and Anglos," by Suzanne Irujo, in *Equity and Choice,* May 1989, reprinted by permission of the Institute for Responsive Education. *Dust Tracks in the Road,* by Zora Neale Hurston, copyright 1996, reprinted by permission of the University of Illinois Press, Champaign, IL. *Finding the Middle Ground: Insights and Application of the Value Orientations Method,* by Kurt Russo, copyright 2000, reprinted by permission of Intercultural Press, Yarmouth, ME. *Gifts Differing,* by Isabel Briggs Myers and Peter B. Myers, copyright 1985, reprinted by permission of Consulting Psychologists Press, Inc. (Modified and reproduced by special permission of the Publisher, Davies-Black Publishing, a division of Consulting Psychologists Press, Inc., Palo Alto, CA 94303 from *Gifts Differing* by Isabel Briggs Myers with Peter B. Myers. Copyright 1980 (original Edition), 1995 by Davies-Black Publishing, a division of Consulting Psychologists Press, Inc. All rights reserved. Further reproduction is prohibited without the Publisher's written consent.) *God Is Red: A Native View of Religion,* by Vine Deloria, Jr., copyright 1973, reprinted by permission of Fulcrum Publishing, Inc., Golden, CO. *In a Different Voice: Psychological Theory and Women's Development,* by Carol Gilligan, copyright 1993, reprinted by permission of Harvard University Press, Cambridge, MA. *The Little Prince,* by Antoine de Saint-Exupéry, copyright 1943 and renewed 1971 by Harcourt, Inc., reprinted by permission of the publisher. *Making Contact,* by Virginia Satir, copyright 1976, reprinted by permission of Celestial Arts, Berkeley, CA.

ABOUT THE AUTHOR

ANN SCHAUBER is the diversity leader for the Oregon State University Extension Service. She holds a Ph.D. from the Union Institute. Previously, Ann worked in Delaware and Michigan with the Cooperative Extension Service. In spite of all her formal education, she credits her two teenage children as her greatest teachers. She lives in McMinnville, Oregon.

INTRODUCTION

This book is about effective intercultural communication in our daily lives. Intercultural communication is person-to-person communication between people from differing cultural backgrounds. These differences affect the meaning of the messages sent and received by people.

Culture is defined more broadly in this book than the way most of us usually think about it. Here, as in the field of intercultural communication, culture refers not only to art, language, food, and artifacts, but more so to the norms, beliefs, and values that we have learned from the many groups that shape our identity. These norms, beliefs, and values affect our perceptions, attitudes, and assumptions about the meaning of what is being communicated.

What this book attempts to do is to give you, the reader, an overall picture of how meanings of messages can vary with differing cultures—along with ways that you can begin to understand a person's intended meaning in a message.

This book is designed so that you can open it anywhere and begin to learn. You might read it through once and then go back to some sections to deepen your understanding. Another approach is to use this book as a tool in specific situations, such as when you are in conflict with someone. Chapter 5 will help you recognize the value and communication style differences that might be contributing to the conflict.

 There are five sections in this book. Section One sets the stage by considering why we would want to work with difference. I describe the process of learning to work with cultural differences as developing an inquiring mind set, an open heart set, and an evolving skill set.

Section Two (Chapters 2 through 7) presents the *mind set*—ways to think about difference. Chapters 2 and 3 describe the self as a cultural self. Chapter 4 introduces the intercultural communication model. Chapter 5 discusses ranges of values and communication styles. Chapter 6 explains how differing cultural groups interact, while Chapter 7 focuses on power dynamics.

Although the material in Section Two is complex, I have attempted to present it in an easy-to-read format so you can use it as a reference when working with others. The intent is to introduce concepts related to cultural difference and to point you toward more in-depth learning opportunities.

Section Three describes the *open heart set*. Chapter 8 focuses on commitment, caring, and emotions.

Section Four integrates the mind set and heart set into a *skill set*. Chapter 9 introduces the skills needed to communicate effectively across cultures, and Chapter 10 describes how to put the skills together in a cross-cultural interaction. Chapter 11, for me, is the most powerful part of this book. Here you will feel and hear the experiences of others. In this chapter, you can practice applying your evolving skill set. I am most grateful to those who shared their experiences so openly. Their stories are a gift to us all.

Finally, in Section Five, Chapter 12 suggests ways to continue your learning experience. Chapter 13 describes a vision of what communities would be like if we all had an inquiring mind set, open heart set, and evolving skill set for working with cultural differences.

I am indebted to all of the scholars who have uncovered the intercultural communication elements described here. I have chosen not to cite those sources within the text for ease of reading. All of the sources are cited in the reference section.

Applying the knowledge and skills described in this book has strengthened the most important relationships in my life and has helped me relate more effectively with others who are very different from me. My hope is that this book will be a catalyst for wonderful intercultural experiences, thus leading to new solutions to challenges at home, at work, and in all of your communities.

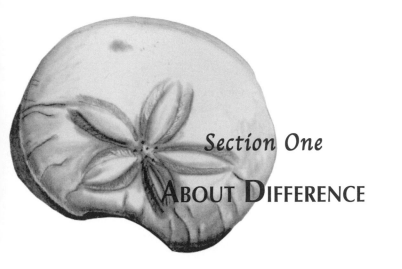

Section One

ABOUT DIFFERENCE

Chapter 1   Why Work with Differences
in Communities?

...until justice rolls down
like waters and righteousness
like a mighty stream.

Dr. Martin Luther King, Jr.

Chapter 1

WHY WORK WITH DIFFERENCES IN COMMUNITIES?

All communities have problems involving the way people get along with one another.

Have you ever thought…

If I were in charge of the world,
I could solve this
problem easily!

At times, a solution to a community problem might seem clear to you. Why doesn't everyone else see it the same way?

Because others are busy thinking the same thing, except that their ideas for solving the problem are different from yours.

Seeing the world from your own perspective to the exclusion of other perspectives is called ethnocentrism.

We all are ethnocentric, some more so than others. We believe that our way of thinking, feeling, and acting is the right way. Some of us believe that our right way is the only way for all people.

The first key to resolving community problems, in a way that includes others who see the world differently, is to step out of our ethnocentrism.

This does not mean we must give up who we are or what we believe.

It does mean adding more ways to see the problem and more possible solutions. We step into others' ways of thinking, feeling, and acting.

We can learn more than one way of seeing the world. There is much more to see than simply our own view.

Si l'on veut savoir la verité,
ouvre ton coeur.

(If you want to know the
truth, open your heart.)

Antoine de Saint-Exupéry
Le Petit Prince
(The Little Prince)

After all, researchers say we use only a small part of our brain capacity. We have lots of room to add new learning to our knowledge bank.

We will encounter internal and external struggles along the way. Working with differences is not easy. We will face our vulnerability and live with moments of uncertainty. The new insights gained and the new possibilities for solutions make the effort worthwhile.

It is not too much to hope that wider and deeper understanding of the gifts of diversity may eventually reduce the misuse and non-use of those gifts. It should lessen the waste of potential, the loss of opportunity, and the number of dropouts and delinquents....

Isabel Briggs Myers
Gifts Differing

Why bother to work with differences? We find answers to this question in our history, in listening to the voices of others, and in our experiences with culturally different others.

- In communities, a group of people makes the rules—from their own cultural values and beliefs—for how the community is to function. I call this group the "dominant" culture because its members have the power to decide the rules that affect others. These "rules" mostly include informal social expectations and might include laws. The structures and processes for participation in the community are governed by the rules. (*Example:* "We start our meetings on time.") Those who have to live by these rules but do not have power to make them are called "nondominant" cultures.

- In communities that are not inclusive, people from the dominant culture feel respected, are heard, and have the opportunity to develop and share their talents.

- People from nondominant cultures, however, feel their voices are not heard, so they shut down, both internally and externally.

- People from the dominant culture wonder why the others are not participating.

- The talents and gifts of people who are not included are left unshared, because the dominant culture structures for participation in community do not provide access for nondominant members.

Thus, when we can work with cultural differences effectively, the voices of those who are excluded can be heard, understood, and respected, and their perspectives can offer new approaches to addressing community issues.

The moral and ethical values of our nation—that all are created equal, with equal rights and responsibilities—call upon us as good citizens to work together.

Furthermore, we are members of a global society. We share a responsibility for maintaining a peaceful life on the planet. Our survival depends on it.

Finally, for each of us, learning about cultural differences is an opportunity to add excitement, adventure, and intrigue to our lives!

Successfully working with differences involves four essential principles:

- I must believe that each person has a special talent or gift to share.

- The only person I can change is myself.

- By opening myself to thinking, feeling, and acting in a way that allows others' gifts to be shared, I create more possibilities for resolving community problems.

- Dominant-culture structures that are in place must be examined and possibly changed to create accessibility for nondominant members.

Negroes should be permitted to dress only in coarse stuffs.... Every distinction should be created between the whites and the Negroes, calculated to make the latter feel the superiority of the former.

Grand jury presentation
Charleston, South Carolina
October 1822

Throughout history, some people have been (and still are) seen as:

- subservient

- having less important needs

- having little value

- lacking worth as full members of society

When we approach difference from the four essential principles listed on page 17, we see others as:

- equal

- having needs as important as our own

- adding value

- worthy of respect and dignity

- unique

- having perceptions and experiences that are different from our own and equally valid

Human beings draw close to one another by their common nature, but habits and customs keep them apart.

Confucian saying

While this book focuses on our differences, it is just as important to know that in many ways we all are the same. For example, we all have certain needs in common. They include the need to:

- survive

- be physically and emotionally safe

- have a sense of belonging, a connection to a group

- be loved and valued

- feel respected, heard, and understood

- be important

- have a sense of predictability

- make a contribution through our work

- make sense out of life and give our personal story meaning

- have a sense of creativity and a renewal of our spirits

Although each of us strives to meet these common needs, there are fundamental differences across cultural groups in how we think, feel, and act in our attempt to meet these common needs.

How can we acknowledge and respect both our commonalities and our differences?

We can suspend judgment of others and become curious about understanding the interaction between them and ourselves.

We all look through our own cultural lenses. What we observe in our surroundings comes through our lenses and becomes part of our internal self-talk. This self-talk can be positive or negative.

We need to recognize that how we interpret what we see through our cultural lenses affects our own emotions and our attitudes toward others. For example, I see a man with an earring in the upper part of his ear. My culture has taught me that men don't pierce their ears. My internal talk is, "Ugh, he must be really weird." My corresponding emotions are feelings of discomfort and anxiety in his presence.

Or, I see a man with an earring in the upper part of his ear. I know that these days more men pierce their ears. My internal talk is, "I see he is wearing an earring. Interesting. I wonder what he is communicating with this jewelry—his individuality? His artistic self? Or he just likes jewelry?" My corresponding emotion is a positive sense of curiosity.

The key here is to become conscious of this internal flow of thoughts and feelings.

We do this by developing an...

 inquiring mind set

 open heart set

 evolving skill set

Communities come in all shapes and sizes. For the purposes of this book, a "community" might be:

- an extended family group

- a neighborhood or town

- a work group

- a church group

- a play group

- a study group

A community exists wherever and however a group of people comes together for a common purpose.

An inclusive community offers a welcoming environment where all who share in the community's purpose feel invited, safe, accepted, respected, included, heard, and understood.

The most effective way to create an inclusive community is to begin with yourself and to develop an inquiring mind set, open heart set, and evolving skill set.

An **inquiring mind set** concerns how we *think* about difference. This includes an understanding of various verbal and nonverbal communication styles and values, along with awareness of the many existing stumbling blocks that prevent nondominant culture members from fully participating in the community.

An **open heart set** concerns how we *feel* about difference and involves appreciating others as they are, no matter how different or similar.

An **evolving skill set** consists of continually learning new ways to *interact* with others who are different from us.

Together, all three shape how we create meaning for ourselves and in our daily interactions with others.

Section Two

THE INQUIRING MIND SET

There is an underlying,
hidden level of culture
that is highly patterned—
a set of unspoken, implicit
rules of behavior and
thought that controls
everything we do.

Edward T. Hall
The Dance of Life: The Other Dimension of Time

Chapter 2

THE SELF AS A CULTURAL SELF

Every one of us is a cultural person. Just as a frame around a painting focuses attention and brings out the features of the painting, a frame around the self can focus attention and bring out the features of an individual. This frame around the self is our culture.

Our cultural frame includes language, art and artifacts, traditions, and social customs. It also goes much deeper. Culture includes norms, beliefs, values, and universal human needs.

Culture is like water to the fish, essential yet not often noticed until the fish is taken out of the water. Culture gives context and continuity to our movements and, like water, buoyancy to our world.

Our culture is...

- learned

- shared

- internalized

- handed down to the next generation

...often without conscious
awareness that we are doing so.

The image of an iceberg is one way to begin to understand culture.

Our culture is like an iceberg. Part of our culture is visible above the water: our language, art and artifacts, food, and customs.

But there is much more below the water's surface! In fact, the visible part of our culture is only the **tip** of the iceberg. Underneath, we find the meanings of our symbols, our norms, beliefs, and values. Way down deep, we find our universal human needs (page 21). It is this larger part of our culture, which often lies outside of conscious awareness, that influences our understanding of "what is."

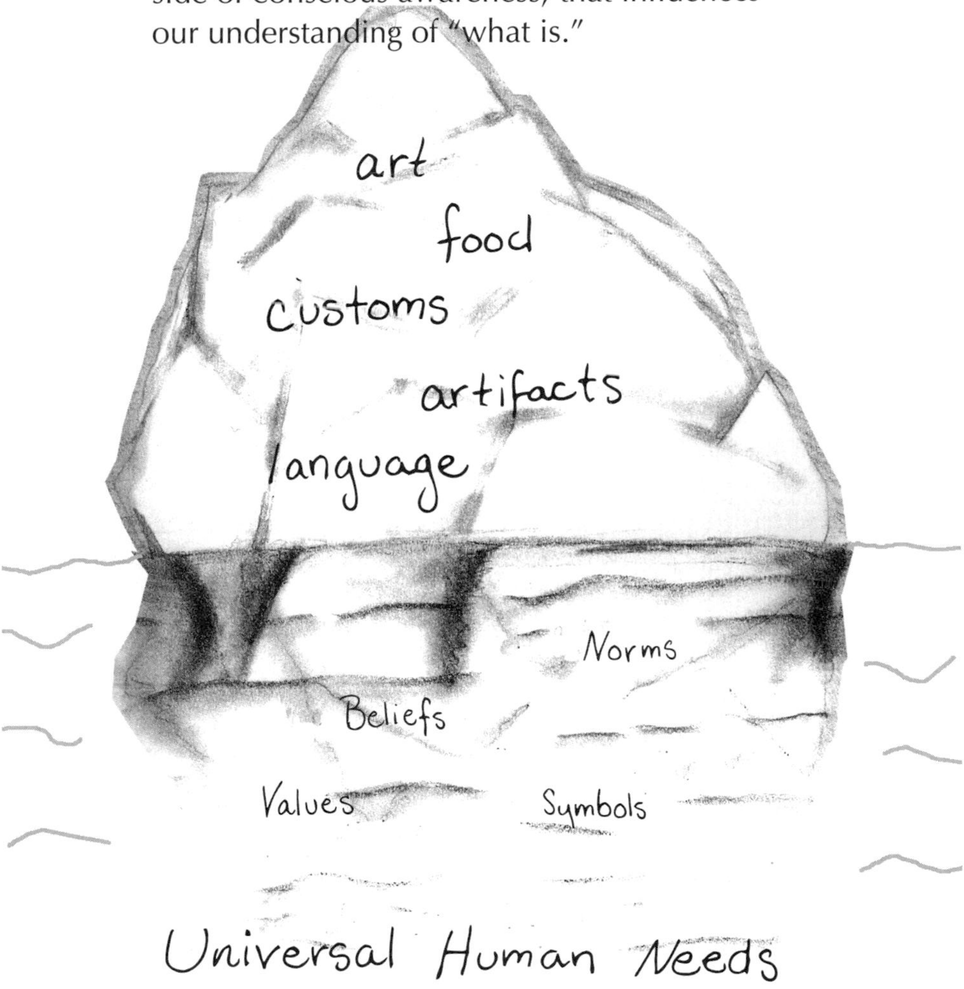

art

food

customs

artifacts

language

Norms

Beliefs

Values

Symbols

Universal Human Needs

Because these hidden parts of ourselves often differ from culture to culture, we find ourselves colliding with the "unknown" and not understanding the cultural patterns of others— something like what happened to the Titanic!

The "underwater" part of culture often is just outside of our conscious awareness. We see, feel, and act based on our norms, beliefs, and values, but we rarely are aware of doing so. It is like breathing. We do not reflect on each breath. We just breathe, taking it for granted.

Because so much of our cultural self is above the surface, it is easy to assume that's all there is. Becoming conscious of all that lies below the surface can be daunting.

The key to developing an inquiring mind set is to seek to become aware of the part of our culture that is below the surface. Once we are aware of how we have internalized the patterns of our cultural upbringing and experiences, we are better able to understand how we make meaning and take action in our world.

This understanding of our cultural self is an ongoing discovery. To uncover who we are culturally takes time, experiences with those who are different, and self-reflection.

Remember, an essential principle in working successfully with difference is:

The only person I can change is myself.

We begin by becoming aware of the norms we live by, our beliefs, and our values. We listen to ourselves to become aware of our perceptions, attitudes, and assumptions. Only then can we begin to understand how others might be different—and how we can interact successfully with those differences.

What are some of the "underwater" aspects of culture?

Norms are the unwritten rules we live by.

Beliefs are what we see as truth.

Values are what we hold to be worth-while and most important.

Perceptions are what we believe we see.

Attitudes are what we feel about what we see.

Assumptions are what we believe about what we see.

As a cultural self, each of us has a set of norms, beliefs, and values. We learn them from our cultural groups. How we perceive the actions and appearances of others, the attitudes we form, and the assumptions we make are all based on these internalized parts of our culture.

We all belong to many cultural groups. How much we identify with a cultural group varies with our life experiences.

What are these cultural groups that shape our view of the world? Many of us think of cultural groups within the context of ethnicity or national origin. Very few of us think of other aspects of culture. An inquiring mind set incorporates many cultural dimensions into the definition of diversity.

In *Workforce America! Managing Employee Diversity as a Vital Resource,* authors Loden and Rosener outline 14 dimensions of diversity. I call these dimensions *cultural* groups because within each of these categories we have experiences that affect the way we communicate with others.

These cultural groups are:

Age
In what decade were you born? How old do you feel?

Nationality
In what nation were you born? Raised? Emigrated from?

Race
How do you identify yourself racially?

Ethnicity
What is your ethnic background? How strong are your ties to your ethnicity(ies)?

Gender
Which gender(s) do you identify with (male/female/both)?

Sexual orientation
To which sex(es) are you physically attracted? How do you identify yourself (homosexual, heterosexual, bisexual, transgendered)?

Physical/ mental abilities	Do you see yourself now or in the past as being physically/ mentally able or with physical/ mental limitations?
Income	How would you define your socioeconomic status now? When you were growing up?
Education	What is your level of formal/ informal education?
Family	What is your marital and parental situation? Children? Siblings? Significant others or partners?
Work experience	What has your work or profession been during most of your career?
Religion	What, if any, would you describe as your religion?
Geographic location	Where do you live? Where have you lived?
Military experience	What, if any, is the extent of your military experience?

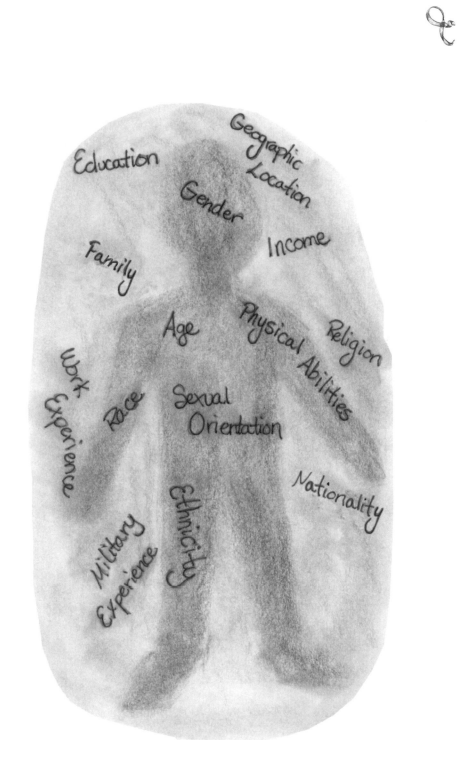

Can you think of other cultural groups?

As you consider where you fit within each of these groups, you will begin to bring your cultural self into awareness. One approach is to reflect on the following questions for each of the cultural group dimensions.

- How would I describe myself within this cultural group?

- How strongly do I identify with each cultural group?

- Which of my norms, beliefs, and values come from each cultural group?

- What perceptions, attitudes, and assumptions might I hold about those who are different from myself within each cultural group?

Write your cultural groups in and around the figure on the next page. You might write the ones you identify with most inside and those that you identify with more loosely outside of the figure.

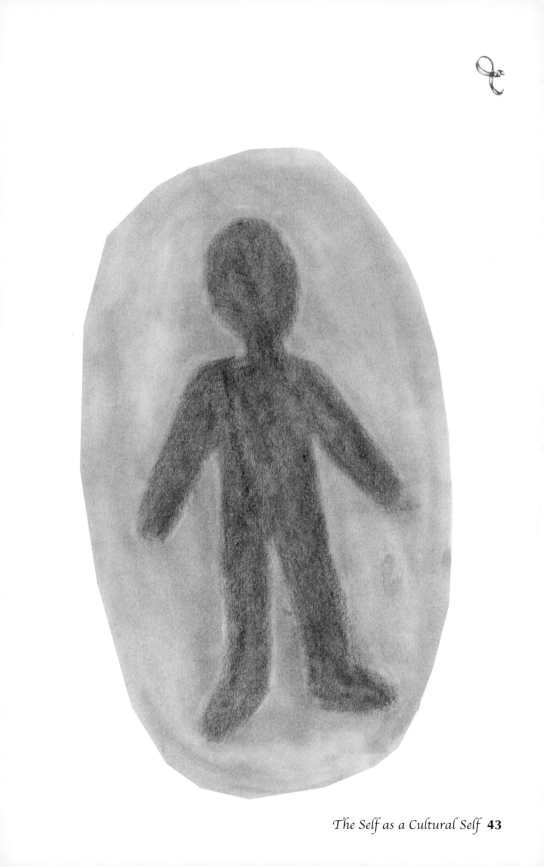

People in a cultural group share common assumptions about right and wrong that shape the way they see, feel, and act. **Not** belonging to a particular cultural group—for example, not having military experience—also shapes our view of how we should behave in the world.

Consider the cultural dimension of work experience. Norms created by the dominant culture say that the professional staff works until the job is done; the secretarial staff works from 8 to 5. Think of the tension that occurs when a member of the professional staff shows up at 10 a.m. The secretary had to get two kids ready for school, pack lunches, and make it to work by 8 a.m. What happens when a professional needs a package mailed on Tuesday, but the secretary runs out of time and mails the package on Wednesday?

Diversity is about all of the ways we are culturally different. It includes each of the cultural dimensions listed here as well as
others—not just race and ethnicity.

As you think about your own culture, notice
that sometimes it is difficult to identify the
norms, beliefs, and values that connect you to
each cultural group. Remember the image of
the iceberg. You are digging into the deeper
part of yourself, the part that probably is not
in your conscious awareness.

To become conscious of this deeper cultural
self is an ongoing process. As you journey
through each day, try paying attention to the
norms, beliefs, and values that guide your
thoughts, feelings, and actions at any given
moment. Try to name the norm, belief, or
value. This is an important part of the process
of becoming aware of your own culture.

Diversity is not about
them, it is about us!

Terry Owens

Chapter 3

OUR CURRENT POINT OF VIEW
PERCEPTIONS, ATTITUDES, ASSUMPTIONS

Our culture surrounds us like a bubble. It gives a sense of meaning to our world as well as safety and security. It also gives us only one way—our culture's "right way"—of seeing the world. Is there more to see?

Take a look at the drawing below. What is represented here? Ask four others what they think it is. Does everyone see the same thing, or do you get many different answers?

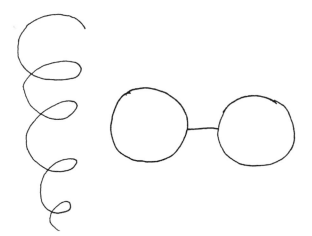

Clearly, there is more than one way to interpret what we see. What we see is based on our cultural filters. It is as if we were wearing cultural eyeglasses. Our norms, beliefs, and values create the prescription for our glasses. When we look through our cultural eyeglasses, certain things are obvious, and others are irrelevant to us.

These cultural filters limit the range of our perceptions, attitudes, and assumptions.

What do you see in this classic picture by cartoonist W.B. Will? Do you see a woman? Does she look young or old?

This is a case where there are two interpretations. One is as correct as the other.

What is depicted in the following picture? Is there more than one interpretation? Chalices? Faces?

What about the figure below?

People only see what they are prepared to see.

Ralph Waldo Emerson

Sometimes we need to be open to new ways of looking at what is in front of us. Consider the picture below. What do you see?

Now turn the picture sideways. Do you see something different?

Sometimes there is more than one valid answer to the question, "What do you see?"

We usually think we know the right way to see what is before us. What happens when there is more than one way to interpret what we see?

Sometimes, when someone sees a reality different from our own, we might even accuse that person of lying!

Encountering another person's point of view can be very unsettling, especially if it is very different from our own set of norms, values, and beliefs.

There is a tendency to defend our view of what is right. We want to be secure and to make sense of our experience.

Thus, over time, many of us develop attitudes and assumptions that support the way we perceive the world—our "right" way. We think and feel that what we perceive is true, and we make judgments about what we see, often without adequate evidence.

Our attitudes and assumptions keep our automatic responses to the world intact. They also keep us from seeing things that do not fit our sense of meaning.

The story on the next page is an example of how our attitudes and assumptions affect our behavioral responses.

A Story

When the Mexican workers started to live in our town, they used to hang out around a pickup in the shopping center near the grocery store. They were all men and they spent their weekend afternoons talking and laughing together in the parking lot. My women friends were afraid to go to the grocery store because they had to walk by the men around the truck. They saw them as loitering and were afraid that the men would harm them in some way.

Another woman friend had lived in Mexico for a year. When she saw the men hanging around the truck, she thought of how Mexicans like to gather in the center of town in their free time to enjoy each others' company. It is a form of relaxation to be together in the outdoors with friends. She was not afraid when she saw them. She knew that this was their new center of town in the United States.

Recognizing that the only person I can change is myself, we now have three steps to working with difference effectively:

- Become aware of myself as a person with a culture.

- Become aware of how my cultural groups have shaped how I understand and act in my world.

- Become aware of how my attitudes and assumptions influence my perceptions and recognize how they can blind me to seeing other possibilities.

After all, what is reality anyway?
Nothin' but a collective hunch.

Jane Wagner
The Search for Signs of
Intelligent Life in the Universe

Next, we must expand our mind set.

This involves moving from simplicity (one way, the way I know) to a place of more complexity (there are many ways, and we need to choose one that works for our situation).

In doing so, we move from clarity to ambiguity. The right way no longer is defined so easily. Things get complicated. This is messy work!

Moving from an attitude of simplicity to one of more complexity can be described as a five-stage learning process.

Stage 1 is to see only one way.

One way, my way..........

Example: The only people who are saved are those in my religion. All others are lost.

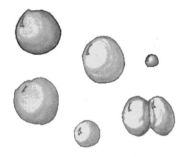

Stage 2 is to see many possibilities, but still one ultimate right.

Many ways..........
*..........Mine, yours, his, hers, theirs—they all are different, but mine is the **one** best way.*

Example: Communism, socialism, and democracy are all forms of government, but democracy is the best way to govern.

Stage 3 is to see many possibilities; your way might be different from mine.

> *What is right for me might be wrong for you..........*
> *..........What is wrong for me might be right for you.*

Example: I am attracted to males, not females. My female friend is attracted to females, not males. I am OK with her attraction to females, but it is not for me.

Stage 4 is to recognize that there is a way that fits each context and situation.

> *My way................................Your way*
> (Dominant group)..................(Nondominant group)

a right way for this situation
(usually the dominant group's way)

Example: We each can practice the religion of our choice in our private lives. In school, however, the right way is to not practice religion at all.

Stage 5 is to see that together we can create a way that fits our context and situation. We come together in respect, listen to one another's views, and work together to agree on a best approach for this situation. What is right is not absolute. It varies with the context and situation, i.e., the time and place.

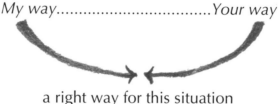

My way..................................Your way

a right way for this situation
(a mutually created approach)

Example: I believe meetings should start on time. You have a different sense of time and often do not arrive at the appointed time because you get into conversations on your way to meetings. We agree to mutually adapt to each other's sense of time. Some of us might not be present when a meeting starts. When we start the meeting, we record notes on a wall chart so that those who arrive later can quickly learn what is happening without disturbing the group.

What stage we are in might vary with the situation in which we find ourselves. For example, I might be in Stage 5 at work and Stage 2 when I visit the people with whom I grew up.

How do we move through these stages? How do we come to see more than one right way? How can we agree on a way that works for all in an inclusive community?

We can begin by learning effective intercultural communication skills.

Chapter 4

THE INTERCULTURAL COMMUNICATION MODEL

When we look at an intercultural communication interaction, we begin to see how challenging it is to understand each other.

Even when two people speak the same language, there often is a difference between what is meant and what is understood, because…

- Nonverbal cues carry most of a message's meaning.

- The same nonverbal cues have different meanings in different cultures.

- Messages are framed (sent) and interpreted (received) through the sender's and receiver's norms, beliefs, and values.

- Norms, beliefs, and values vary by culture.

- Messages are filtered twice through perceptions, attitudes, and assumptions— once through the sender's filters and once through the receiver's filters.

Trying to communicate effectively is like putting two icebergs next to each other and asking them to understand each other. Out of the
depths come the universal human needs.
Those needs move up to the surface, however, through differing values, beliefs, and
norms, which you cannot see. All you can see
is the top of the iceberg.

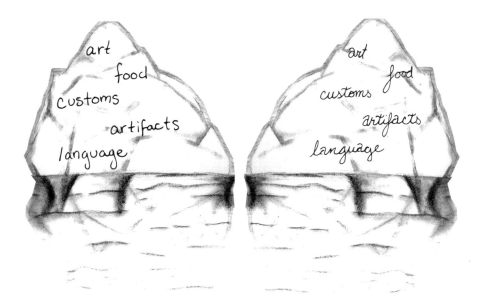

Recognizing the complexity of communication, the key to effective communication is to complete the communication circle by checking for meaning.

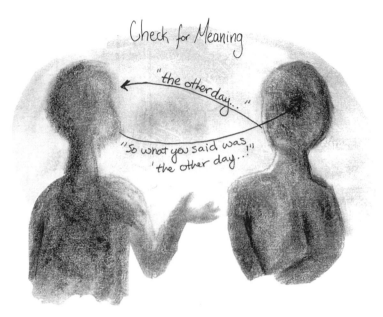

To check for meaning in intercultural communication, we must understand:

- how to observe with openness

- different value systems

- the meanings of different communication styles

- how to respond skillfully

This involves:

- adding to our mind set

- expanding our skill set

What each of us wants in communicating with others is to feel respected, valued, understood, and accepted for who we are.

Chapter 5

ADDING TO OUR MIND SET
FRAMES FOR SEEING DIFFERENCES

We can think of our mind set as a series of frames of reference, like a photo gallery. The gallery of pictures we present in this chapter is intended to help you learn about differences. This knowledge will be useful when you are involved in or observe interpersonal exchanges.

A major task remains for Western man. He must quickly come to grips with the breadth of human experiences and understand these experiences from a world viewpoint, not simply a Western one.

Vine Deloria, Jr.
God Is Red: A Native View of Religion

Scholars such as Edward T. Hall, Florence Kluckhohn, and Geert Hofstede have identified differences in values and communication styles among cultural groups. An awareness of these differences can help us understand others' experiences.

The cultural difference gallery includes:

A. **view of the self**

B. **values**

C. **communication styles: context, verbal, and nonverbal**

D. **sense of personal physical space**

E. **sense of time**

We will look at each of these cultural frames of reference as a range, or continuum, of possibilities, ranging between two contrasting characteristics. As you read about each continuum, think about where you see yourself. Where do you see others?

To be effective communicators, it is helpful to make these frames part of the mind set we use in making sense of what is being communicated. They expand our possibilities for seeing and understanding accurately.

In this chapter, we begin with one over-arching frame—one's view of the self—and then move into value and communication frames, including sense of personal space and time.

A caveat: The following pages give a broad-brush review of the rich literature on value and communication style differences. This review is not intended to provide a deep understanding of these differences. The intent is to introduce the concepts and to stimulate your curiosity to learn more. (See Chapter 12 for suggestions.) These pages also are meant to encourage you to become observant of these differences in your daily life.

It takes study, observation, and reflection to begin to grasp the richness of these differences. First, we must identify the differences and begin to see them around us. Then, we can begin to incorporate them into our mind set.

Remember that we are presenting ranges, or continuums, of differences. An individual can fall anywhere along a continuum. Few fall at either extreme. A person's location on a continuum can vary with the context, situation, and time.

Certain cultural groups generally occupy a certain position on a continuum. This does not mean that everyone in the group is the same, however. Until we know a person well, we cannot know his or her cultural values and communication styles.

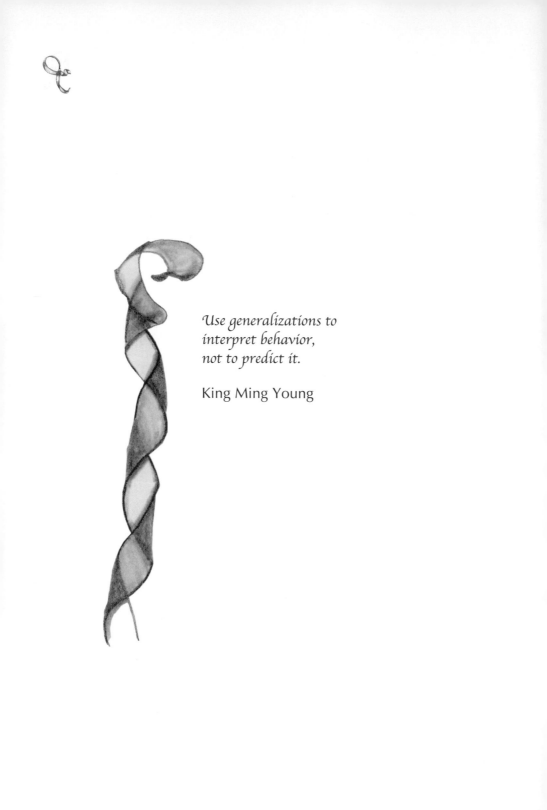

Use generalizations to interpret behavior, not to predict it.

King Ming Young

Consider the bell curve. Within a cultural group, we are likely to find individuals scattered all over the continuum. When we make a generalization about a group, we are referring to where the majority of the people fall on the continuum.

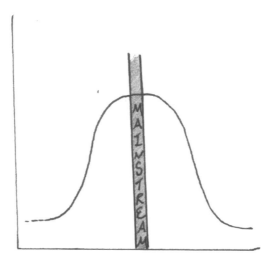

These frames of reference increase our possibility of seeing, in a nonjudgmental way, more of what is being communicated. They broaden our awareness from only one way (my way) to the rich variety of many possible ways.

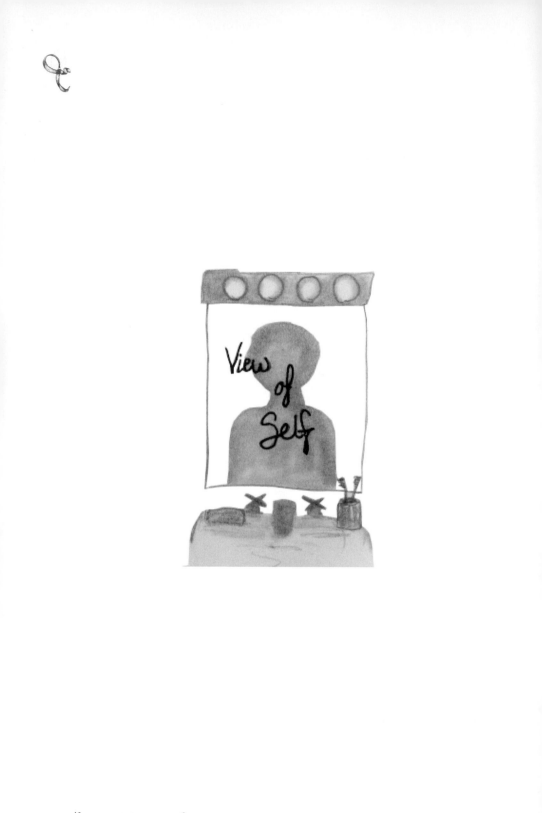

A. View OF THE SELF

One overarching frame of reference is one's perception of the self. This perception varies across cultures.

One's definition of self ranges from:

Independent self   **Interdependent self**

← ————————————————————————————— →

Focus on "I"   Focus on "We"

If I am not for myself,
who will be for me?

Talmud: Aboth 1:14

The independent self:

- sees the self as separate from others.

- behaves according to personal needs.

- believes in the rights of individuals.

- has personal goals that might or might not be the same as those of family or group goals.

- might have many short-term relationships over a lifetime.

The voice of the independent self says:

- I have a right to ask questions.

- I must stand up for my own rights.

- I want life to be fair for me and everyone.

It is as if I have a string tied from my belly-button to the belly-button of every member of my family. Every move I make affects them.

Dr. Sheri Sinaga
Malaysian-American

The interdependent self:

- sees the self as interconnected with others.

- behaves based on the needs of the family group.

- considers personal goals to be the same as family goals.

- believes in loyalty and cooperation with one's group.

- might have a few close, lifelong relation-ships.

- sees the extended family as the primary group.

The voice of the interdependent self says:

- No questions asked.

- We do as we are taught.

Examples

Independent self **Interdependent self**

"I" "We"
U.S. Americans of Asians
western European heritage

In the United States, generally, Native Americans, African-Americans, Mexican- and Latino-Americans tend to be more interdependent than Americans of western European heritage.

Women tend to be more interdependent than men.

Groups with a predominantly independent view of the self may prefer that aging grandparents live in an assisted care facility, while groups with a predominantly interdependent self may prefer that aging grandparents live with the families of their grown children.

When young adults graduate from high school in an independent-self culture, they usually are expected to leave home and begin a life on their own. In an interdependent-self culture, there usually is no expectation for young adults to leave home.

A situation to ponder:

What happens when a child is raised by a culturally inter-dependent family group but receives schooling in a culturally independent environment?

Whether at the bargaining table, in the boardroom, or in the multicultural classroom, it behooves us to make a good-faith effort to understand others' points of view. Entering into the (value) subjectivity of others who are different from us not only breaks down false stereotypes but also serves to humanize a situation by encouraging each side to stretch its view to see from within the orientation of the other. For groups in conflict, this process can elevate the discussion to higher common ground and can replace reflexivity with reasoned, open dialogue.

Kurt Russo
Finding the Middle Ground: Insights and Application of the Value Orientations Method

B. A SPECTRUM OF POSSIBILITIES IN VALUES

Values are the core beliefs that people hold to be most important and right. We only have to dig into our wallets and purses to find evidence of what we value. A picture of my family implies that my immediate family is very important to me. My driver's license represents my freedom and mobility as well as my conformance to the law. What is in your wallet or purse?

Interestingly, our values vary across cultural groups. Borrowing from the work of four scholars, we are able to frame a picture of values across cultures.

As you review these value orientations, can you think of examples that apply to you? Which option do you choose first? Second? How does your choice vary by situation?

Note: This section on value differences is simplified so as to introduce the spectrum of possibilities. The research itself goes much deeper in describing the variations.

Kluckhohn and Strodtbeck's value dimensions

The ground-breaking research of Florence Kluckhohn and Fred Strodtbeck in the south-west U.S. in the 1960s is based on three assumptions:

- All people face common problems.

- There is a limited number of possible values driving the solutions to problems.

- All value orientations are present in all people, but they are preferred differently depending on the situation.

Kluckhohn and Strodtbeck say that cultural groups have primary and secondary value orientations around common aspects of the meaning of life:

- the essential character of human nature

- the proper relationship of people to nature and the supernatural

- sense of time

- how people occupy themselves

- the relationship of humans to other humans

THE ESSENTIAL CHARACTER OF HUMAN NATURE

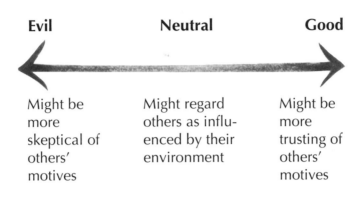

Evil	Neutral	Good
Might be more skeptical of others' motives	Might regard others as influenced by their environment	Might be more trusting of others' motives

The essential character of human nature is viewed by some as unchangeable and by others as changeable. For example, if you are essentially good, you always will be essentially good to those who see essential character as unchangeable. Changeable means that although you are essentially good now, you could become essentially evil later.

Examples

Evil: He intends to hurt me, so I must protect myself.

Neutral: His tough life has made him afraid to love.

Good: He is doing the best job he can.

THE PROPER RELATIONSHIP OF PEOPLE
TO NATURE AND THE SUPERNATURAL

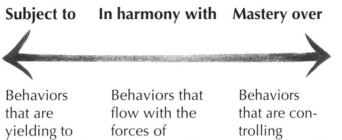

Subject to   **In harmony with**   **Mastery over**

Behaviors that are yielding to the forces of nature and the supernatural

Behaviors that flow with the forces of nature and the supernatural

Behaviors that are controlling of nature and the supernatural

Examples

Subject to: A volcano erupts and destroys a city.

In harmony: Gardening organically.

Mastery: Building dams to make electricity.

Sense of Time as it Relates to Our Lives

Focus on past	Focus on present	Focus on future

← ──────────────────────────── →

Tradition-bound; honors ancestral ties	Situation-bound; honors the moment	Goal-bound; honors plans/ strategies

Examples

Past: My parents choose my marriage partner.

Present: We're in love. Let's live together.

Future: After I get a good job, we'll get married.

How people occupy themselves

Being	Being in becoming	Doing

← ———————————————————————— →

Expressive; focus is on emotional vitality	Attention to inner development; focus is on spiritual renewal	Action-oriented; focus is on achievement

Examples

Being: Sitting in the coffee shop all morning with friends

Being in becoming: Meditating every day

Doing: Deciding to become the top executive

THE RELATIONSHIP OF HUMANS TO OTHER HUMANS

Class/caste	Group	Individual

Obligations are passed from genera-tion to generation, authoritarian decision-making, strong social class and/or caste divisions	Extended fam-ily ties, group decision-making, group interdepen-dence	Emphasis on individual's unique qualities, autonomous decision-making, individual independence

Examples

Class/caste: You must wear a coat and tie to eat here.

Group: I will bring my family here to eat.

Individual: Where would you like to eat tonight?

Think about the sense of self as interdependent or independent and apply each value set to this view of self. For example, within a class/caste system, interdependence is most obvious among people in the same social class. People do not associate with, or have close ties with, people outside their class.

On the other hand, people with an independent sense of self feel free to associate with others regardless of their class or social situation.

Values are among the first things children learn—not consciously, but implicitly. Development psychologists believe that by the age of 10, most children have their basic value system firmly in place, and after that age, changes are difficult to make. Because they were acquired so early in our lives, many values remain unconscious to those who hold them.

Geert Hofstede
Cultures and Organizations: Software of the Mind

Geert Hofstede's value dimensions

Geert Hofstede, a researcher from the Nether-lands, studied data from surveys of IBM employees in 50 different countries from 1968 to 1972. He identified four value dimensions that varied across national cultures:

- *power distance:* large to small

- *power of the group:* individualistic to group-oriented

- *uncertainty avoidance:* low to high

- *assertiveness of societies:* masculine to feminine

Where do you see yourself in each of these value dimensions?

POWER DISTANCE

Large   **Small**

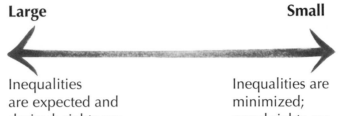

Inequalities   Inequalities are
are expected and   minimized;
desired; rights are   equal rights are
based on privi-   expected
lege and status

Power distance is the extent to which less
powerful members of families, schools, communities, and workplaces expect and
accept an unequal distribution of power.
Think about the differences in power
between…

- a boss and a secretary

- a parent and a child

- a principal and a teacher

Norms—large power distance

At work   Bosses have authority.

At home   Parents are treated with respect and obedience.

At school   Teachers have wisdom and authority.

Norms—small power distance

At work   Bosses include workers in democratic decision-making.

At home   Parents treat children as equals.

At school   Students take initiative.

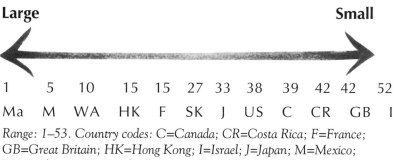

COUNTRY RANKING—POWER DISTANCE

Large   **Small**

1	5	10	15	15	27	33	38	39	42	42	52
Ma	M	WA	HK	F	SK	J	US	C	CR	GB	I

Range: 1–53. Country codes: C=Canada; CR=Costa Rica; F=France; GB=Great Britain; HK=Hong Kong; I=Israel; J=Japan; M=Mexico; Ma=Malaysia; SK=South Korea; US=United States; WA=West Africa

POWER OF THE GROUP

Resides in the individual

Resides in the group

Who I am reflects my own accomplishments

Who I am reflects my family or my identity group

In individualistic societies, ties between individuals are loose. Each person takes care of self and immediate family.

Communication is respected if it is direct, specific, and gets to the point quickly. People are expected to say what they mean and be honest. Wrongdoing results in guilt and loss of self-respect for the individual.

In group-oriented societies, individuals are born into tight extended family groups that protect everyone in the group in exchange for strong group loyalty.

Communication is high-context (page 113). People try to maintain harmony and avoid confrontation. Wrongdoing results in shame for self and family.

Norms—individualistic

At work   Promotion is based on skills.

At home   We consider personal needs and wants.

At school   Education leads to a better job; learning is lifelong, so we must learn how to learn.

Norms—group-oriented

At work   Promotions consider group affiliations, network systems, and family ties.

At home   We consider extended family needs and wants.

At school   Education leads to entry into higher status groups; evidence of learning includes how to be acceptable to group members.

COUNTRY RANKING—POWER OF THE GROUP

Individualistic   **Group-oriented**

1	3	4	10	19	22	32	36	37	39	43	46
US	GB	C	F	I	J	M	Ma	HK	WA	SK	CR

Range: 1–53. Country codes: C=Canada; CR=Costa Rica; F=France; GB=Great Britain; HK=Hong Kong; I=Israel; J=Japan; M=Mexico; Ma=Malaysia; SK=South Korea; US=United States; WA=West Africa

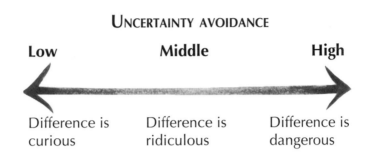

Uncertainty avoidance

Low	Middle	High
Difference is curious	Difference is ridiculous	Difference is dangerous

Uncertainty avoidance is the extent to which a society feels threatened by unknown situations and prefers predictability. This is manifested by a need for rules.

Norms—low level of uncertainty avoidance

At work   We are more tolerant of crazy ideas; rules are less important but are respected.

At home   We are more relaxed about what is inappropriate, dirty, or dangerous.

At school   Teachers might not know all the answers.

Norms—high level of uncertainty avoidance

At work   Follow the rules, work hard, time is money.

At home   We have clear rules about what is inappropriate, dirty, or dangerous.

At school   Teachers have all the right answers.

COUNTRY RANKING—UNCERTAINTY AVOIDANCE

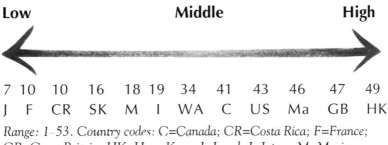

Low						Middle					High
7 10	10	16	18 19	34	41	43	46	47	49		
J F	CR	SK	M I	WA	C	US	Ma	GB	HK		

Range: 1–53. Country codes: C=Canada; CR=Costa Rica; F=France; GB=Great Britain; HK=Hong Kong; I=Israel; J=Japan; M=Mexico; Ma=Malaysia; SK=South Korea; US=United States; WA=West Africa

Assertiveness*

Masculine   **Feminine**

← ——————————————————————————— →

In masculine societies, men are supposed to be tough, assertive, and focused on economic success, while women are expected to be tender, modest, and focused on quality of life. Masculine societies value progress and material success.

*These two terms, masculine and feminine, are Hofstede's terms. The terms are not intended to refer to specific genders (male or female) but rather qualities that Hofstede associates with the terms masculine and feminine. Some educators refer to these variables as tough or tender. I chose to use masculine and feminine because, to me, they are richer in meaning than tough and tender. I acknowledge, however, that the terms can be confusing.

In feminine societies, both women and men are supposed to be focused on quality of life and to be tender and modest. Feminine societies value caring for others.

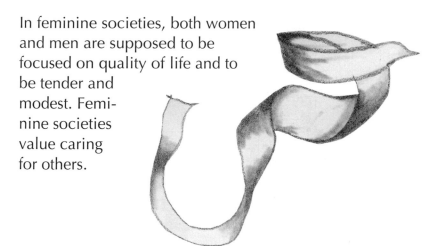

Norms—masculine

At work   Live to work.

At home   Fathers deal with facts, mothers with feelings.

At school   Boys and girls study different subjects; being the best is expected.

Norms—feminine

At work   Work to live.

At home   Both fathers and mothers deal with facts and feelings.

At school   Boys and girls study the same subjects; being average is expected.

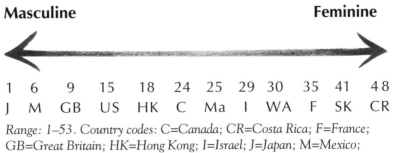

COUNTRY RANKING—ASSERTIVENESS

Masculine											**Feminine**
1	6	9	15	18	24	25	29	30	35	41	4 8
J	M	GB	US	HK	C	Ma	I	WA	F	SK	CR

Range: 1–53. Country codes: C=Canada; CR=Costa Rica; F=France; GB=Great Britain; HK=Hong Kong; I=Israel; J=Japan; M=Mexico; Ma=Malaysia; SK=South Korea; US=United States; WA=West Africa

Michael Bond's value dimension

Michael Bond's addition to our understanding of values comes from an Eastern perspective. Bond, a Canadian who lives and works in Hong Kong, created the Chinese Value Survey and administered it to college students in 23 countries in the 1980s. His results correlated well with Hofstede's value orientations and added one more value dimension, known as Confucian dynamism.

Confucius was an influential philosopher who lived around 500 B.C. in China. His ideas have become ethical lessons for daily life for the Chinese people. The key difference between this Eastern view and a Western view is that the Eastern mind is not in search of an absolute truth. Rather, it is more interested in living a virtuous life.

Confucius' teachings consist of a set of practical guidelines for living in continuous improvement of one's life. Bond explains the principle of living life virtuously within a long-term or short-term orientation to life.

SOCIETY'S ORIENTATION TO LIFE

Long-term   **Short-term**

←――――――――――――――――――――――――→

Members of societies with a long-term orientation:

- organize relationships by status

- are persistent and persevere for slow results

- are thrifty in the use of resources

- have a sense of shame

- are concerned with respecting the demands of virtue

Members of societies with a short-term orientation:

- expect quick results

- feel a pressure to have what others have even if they can't afford it

- expect reciprocation of greetings, favors, and gifts

- are concerned with the truth

COUNTRY RANKING—SOCIETY'S ORIENTATION TO LIFE

Long-term   **Short-term**

2	4	5	17	18	20
HK	J	SK	US	GB	C

Ranking: 1–23. Country codes: C=Canada; GB=Great Britain; HK=Hong Kong; J= Japan; SK=South Korea; US=United States

As we begin to see how values vary across cultures, we begin to realize that what we hold as most important is not the same for all of us.

Even understanding the possible variations in our values doesn't tell us exactly what others value, however. What this information does is give us more possibilities of what the others' values might be. We must engage in dialogue and listen to others to learn what their values are.

When we engage in dialogue, we discover that the communication styles of others also vary. Communication styles are clues to what someone values. For example, a person with a very formal communication style might value a greater power distance than a person with an informal communication style.

The next section describes communication style differences.

C. COMMUNICATION STYLES

Now that we have considered value differences, we can examine how communication styles vary across cultures.

As you explore these variations, consider what values discussed in the previous section underlie each communication style.

Borrowing from the work of Stella Ting-Toomey and Edward T. Hall, the following communication styles can be described:

The communication context

Low .... High

Verbal styles

Direct.. Indirect
Linear .... Circular
Informal .... Formal
Confrontational .... Compliant
Initiating....................................... Listening
Factual .... Intuitive
Rational .... Emotive

Nonverbal styles

Vocalics (e.g., accents, pitch, and volume)
Tone of voice
    Harsh .... *Soft*
Eye contact
    Maintain............*Break off* .... *Avert*
Touching
    Bow.............*Handshake* .... *Continual*

Sense of personal physical space

Close...Distant

Sense of time

Monochronic .... Polychronic

Communication context

Low   **High**

The communication context is low when:

- The meaning of a message is contained in the words.

- The speaker is responsible for communicating a clear, concise message.

- Social norms, roles, and the current situation are not important in carrying the meaning of the message.

- History and current relationship are not important in carrying the meaning of the message.

Low-context communication is direct and is used to emphasize facts, personal thoughts, feelings, and opinions.

"Mommy, I love you!"

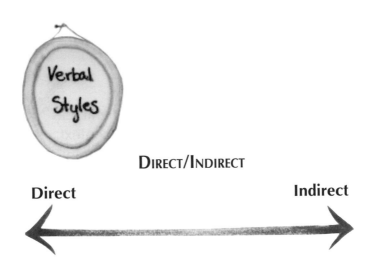

Direct/Indirect

Direct ←————————————→ **Indirect**

Direct communication is when:

- I tell you exactly what I mean.

- My words are explicit.

- I appreciate candidness.

"I want to go out to dinner tonight."

Indirect communication is when:

- I imply my meaning without explaining each part.

- I assume you understand what I mean without telling you everything.

- Candidness can be offensive at inappropriate times and settings.

"I can't think of anything to make for dinner. I've cooked dinner every night this week."

Linear/Circular

Linear   **Circular**

In linear communication, I explicitly tell you what my point is. What I say is what I mean. I want to be clear so you will understand me.

> *"The doctor said I have lung cancer and have 3 months to live."*

In circular communication, I tell you everything around the point without explicitly telling you the point. The point is implied. I respect you; therefore, I know you will understand what I mean. If I were to tell you the point, I would insult your intelligence.

> *"I went to see the doctor, and he upset me so much. Now I have to talk to my family and tell them. I don't know what I am going to do at work. I worry about how much money I have. There is so much left to do to fix my house."*

Understanding context is crucial to understanding circular communication. Context is less important in linear communication.

Circular communication is high-context and seems like pointless rambling to a low-context communicator. Linear communication is low-context and seems blunt to a high-context communicator.

INFORMAL/FORMAL

Informal   **Formal**

Communication is a blend of both verbal and nonverbal messages. On the verbal level, the level of formality is communicated through the words we use. On the nonverbal level, the level of formality is communicated through the actions we use.

In an informal style, a person is greeted by first name even if meeting for the first time; for example, "Hi, Jan, how're you doin'?"

The greeting might be accompanied by a non-verbal gesture such as a smile or hug, depending on the cultural norm. Sometimes there is no verbal greeting, only a nod or smile of recognition.

An informal departure might be "See ya' later!" with an accompanying smile, hug, or wave good-bye. In some cases, there is no verbal acknowledgment of departure.

In a formal style, a person is greeted verbally by title and name, such as "Hello, Dr. Booke" or "Good morning, Doña María. How are you this morning? How is your family?"

This might be accompanied by nonverbal gestures such as a handshake, kiss on the cheek, or hug, depending on the cultural norm.

Departures are also formal: "Good-bye, Dr. Booke. It has been a delight to see you." This also is accompanied by an appropriate nonverbal gesture such as a handshake, kiss, or hug.

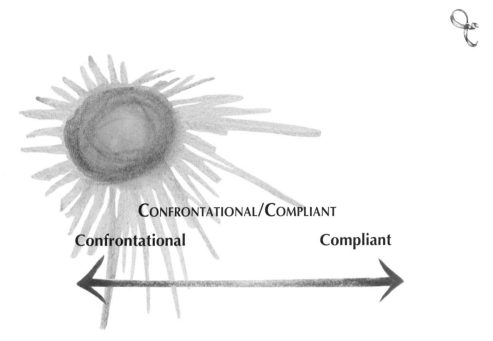

CONFRONTATIONAL/COMPLIANT

Confrontational   **Compliant**

Confrontational style is an emotionally expressive means of asserting one's point of view.

> *"Your dog has been keeping me up all night barking for the last three nights. I need to get some sleep. You need to keep your dog quiet."*

Compliant style is a softer style intended to maintain harmony in the group.

> *"I heard a dog barking loudly last night, so I put in my earplugs."*

Which style do you think is high-context?
Which is low-context?

INITIATING/LISTENING

Initiating   **Listening**

Initiating involves "getting the ball rolling" to solve problems.

> *"Why don't we raise money to build a community center?"*

Listening involves hearing the context of what is being communicated.

> *"You have an interest in bringing the people in this community together?"*

FACTUAL/INTUITIVE

Factual   **Intuitive**

Factual communication describes existing data.

> *"Fifty people are registered for this event."*

Intuitive communication involves describing the situation from an inner contextual sense of what is happening.

> *"I would say that 65 people will show up for this event."*

RATIONAL/EMOTIVE

Rational   **Emotive**

⟵――――――――――――――⟶

Rational style involves a linear, logical approach.

> "It makes sense that this child is not doing well in school because he needs better nutrition."

Emotive style involves feelings.

> "How could anyone allow this child to come to school without a good breakfast?"

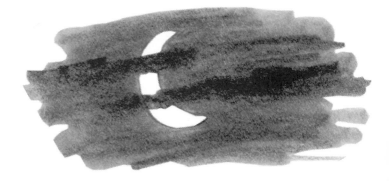

As you communicate with others, you might notice other verbal styles. How would you define these styles on a continuum of difference?

As we reflect on our own communication style and how it varies along the high-context/ low-context continuum, it is important to remember that we learn during childhood the "right" way to deliver our communication messages. Later, it is difficult to change what we internally perceive as good and polite when we interact cross-culturally.

In understanding the
language of a culture, we
hold the key to the heart
of a culture. By under-
standing the nonverbal
nuances, expressions,
styles, and boundaries of
a culture, we enter the
heart of that culture.
Acquiring knowledge is a
good first step when we
are preparing ourselves to
enter into any new
culture. Knowledge
together with mindfulness
can help us to be more in
tune....

Stella Ting-Toomey
Communicating Across Cultures

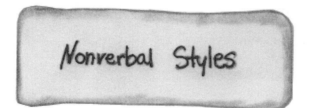

Nonverbal Styles

Each verbal style has associated nonverbal cues. Can you think of nonverbal gestures for each of the verbal styles described above?

Nonverbal messages can be intentional or unintentional. They carry the emotional and attitudinal meaning of the message. When verbal and nonverbal messages are inconsistent, listeners will trust the nonverbal cues to carry the speaker's true intent.

In the remainder of this section, we briefly describe vocalics, tone of voice, eye contact, and touching as nonverbal ways to communicate meaning.

Vocalics

Vocalics include sounds such as:

Perceived accents
Thick .... None
Articulation
Precise .... Slurred
Pitch range
High .... Low
Pitch intensity
Emotional .... Uninvolved
Volume
Loud .... Soft

Vocal signals mean different things in different cultures. Thus, we might judge another's meaning through our ethnocentric filters and miss what the speaker is really communicating.

For example, a native English speaker listening to a conversation among native Chinese speakers will hear a pitch range that sounds like an argument, when, in fact, the Chinese speakers are having a pleasant conversation.

The same goes for the emotive pitch intensity used by Italians and Latino-Americans. A native English speaker might think Italians or Latino-Americans are upset and about to get into a fight, when, in fact, they simply are expressing their emotions! Native English speakers frequently are perceived as cold and unfeeling by Latino-Americans and Italians because their pitch intensity is neutral and uninvolved.

Tone of voice

Tone of voice carries emotional meaning. Tone of voice varies across cultures.

For example, southern Europeans and Arabs prefer emotionally expressive tones. East and Southeast Asians prefer soft, moderating tones. Germans and U.S. Americans prefer to be nonexpressive.

Eye contact

Maintain   **Break off**   **Avert**

←——————————————————————————→

Meanings conveyed by eye contact vary across cultures. The way we use eye contact communicates respect and a sense of whether the listener is paying attention. For example, in the U.S.:

- European-Americans assume that direct eye contact shows respect and means that you are telling the truth and paying attention.

- Members of many high-context cultures such as Asian-Americans, Native Americans, and Latino-Americans tend to avert their eyes as a sign of respect.

- African-Americans tend to maintain eye contact when speaking and break off eye contact when listening, while European-Americans tend to break off eye contact when speaking and maintain eye contact when listening.

Because eye contact can convey several different meanings, it is not reliable as an only cue to determine meaning in a message. Use another cue—verbal or nonverbal—to help you determine the meaning of the message.

Consider this scenario in a U.S. courtroom:

> *The European-American jurors are expecting direct eye contact from the Asian-American giving testimony. To show respect, the Asian-American averts his eyes and does not look directly at the jurors. What do the jurors think?*

Touching

Touching is a powerful means of communicating nonverbally. The message sent by a touch can range from positive to negative. For example, touching can communicate a ritualistic greeting or acknowledgment (handshake), an expression of affection (kiss), playfulness (tickling), or a means of controlling (grabbing).

What touch communicates varies according to national and ethnic cultures, as well as gender and status roles. For example:

- In the United States, hand-holding of same-sex adults often is assumed to mean that the couple is homosexual. Hand-holding among same-sex Arabs is a sign of friendship. Opposite-sex handshakes traditionally are unacceptable for Arabs.

- Generally, European-Americans tend to engage in less touching as a sign of friendship than Latinos. For Latinos, touching the arm or hand while talking is a sign of connection. Generally, Asians do not touch in greetings and departures.

As with all culture-specific examples, not all individuals from a particular cultural group fall within the general tendency of that group.

Next, we examine our sense of space and time as they relate to communication style.

D. Sense of Personal Physical Space

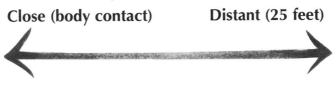

Close (body contact)   **Distant (25 feet)**

Personal physical space meets our needs for security, stability, trust, inclusion, and connection. Personal space varies by culture. Where a person is on this continuum varies according to cultural norms, the context, and the situation.

Edward T. Hall says that European-Americans use four spatial distances:

- *intimate:* from body contact to 18 inches

- *personal:* 18 inches to 4 feet for casual conversations

- *social:* 4 to 12 feet for formal business or social interactions

- *public:* 12 to 25 feet for lectures or performances

Personal space varies among cultures. For example, according to Gary P. Ferraro, the average conversational space is approximately:

- 20 inches for European-Americans

- 14 to 15 inches for some Latino-Americans (Costa Ricans, Puerto Ricans, Jamaicans)

- 9 to 10 inches for Arabs

If a Latino stands only 14 inches away when talking to an American of European descent, the Euro-American might think the Latino is intrusive and rude. Likewise, if a European-American stands 20 inches away when talking to a Latino, the Latino might think the Euro-American is cold and withdrawn.

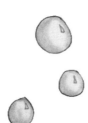

E. Sense of Time

Monochronic   **Polychronic**

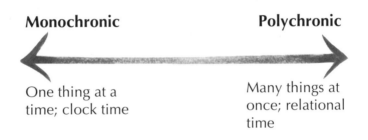

One thing at a   Many things at
time; clock time   once; relational
                        time

Cultural anthropologist Edward T. Hall made
a magical observation while living among the
Navajo and Hopi in the southwest U.S. in the
1930s. The Navajo and Hopi, who do not
even have a word for "time" in their vocabu-
lary, regard time completely differently than
does the dominant U.S. culture.

This discovery led Hall to recognize two completely different ways to perceive time, which
he termed "monochronic" and "polychronic"
time.

Monochronic, or M-time, refers to a preference for doing one thing at a time, often sequentially. Time is compartmentalized, tangible, and linear. Time can be saved, lost, wasted, spent, killed, or running out. M-time is oriented toward schedules, tasks, and procedures. Because monochronic time is compartmentalized, it is possible to concentrate on one thing at a time. M-time is most evident in government, business, schools, sports, and the professional world.

Polychronic, or P-time, refers to being involved in many things at once. Polychronic time revolves around interactions with people rather than schedules and appointments. In P-time, matters remain flexible and changeable; nothing is solid.

Polychronic people tend to be more high-context and have more of an interdependent view of self than do monochronic people. Polychronic people are deeply involved in building and maintaining relationships. Family comes first, close friends and colleagues second, and all other matters are considered in relation to them. In the U.S., we are more likely to find P-time only in the home. In many other countries, polychronic time is the norm.

Whether people behave in a monochronic or polychronic manner varies with the cultural group, context, and situation.

Generally, there is a tendency for:

- women to be more polychronic than men

- Euro-Americans to be more monochronic than Native Americans, Latino-Americans, Asian-Americans, and African-Americans

Those who live according to schedules and have many projects going at once tend to say they are both monochronic and polychronic. They might be right; however, there is a subtle difference between these two concepts of time that can easily be missed.

This concept of time is intertwined with the value set of being and doing. Many people in the dominant U.S. culture work on many tasks at once, but their underlying value is to accomplish many things, commonly known as "multitasking." They accomplish them one at a time, sectioning out the work in short time sequences.

A more polychronic person has an underlying value of being; thus, relationships with others are more important than accomplishing many things. A classic example is a polychronic person working at a deli. While preparing a customer's order, the second, third, and fourth customers arrive, and each engages in conversation with the deli worker. The worker is still preparing the first order, although the first customer might not think so. As a result, a long time passes before the first person is served. If the first customer is more monochronic, he might become upset or impatient, and the deli worker probably won't understand why.

Where would you place yourself on the monochronic–polychronic continuum? Your answer might vary according to context and situation.

Summary

Your culture has given you a set of values and communication styles. Other cultural groups have different values and communication styles. These variations are described within a broad continuum of differences. The primary differences relate to:

- the view of the self as interdependent to independent

- varying value sets that tell us what is right

- verbal communication that is low- to high-context

- varying nonverbal cues that carry most of the meaning of our messages

- varying sense of personal physical space

- two different senses of time

The next two pages present these variables for quick reference. You might want to mark an X where you see yourself on the following continuums. You might also mark an O where you see a colleague or family member who is different from you. Reflecting on where you see yourself on these continuums can lead to insights for more effective communication.

CULTURAL FRAMES OF REFERENCE AT A GLANCE

A. VIEW OF THE SELF

Interdependent .... Independent

B. VALUES

Essential human nature
Evil...........................Neutral .... Good

Humans' relationship to nature/supernatural
Subject to.............Harmony with .... Mastery over

Sense of time as it relates to life
Focus on past ......Focus on present ...... Focus on future

How people occupy themselves
Being...............Being in becoming .... Doing

Human relationships
Class/caste................Group...................... Individual

Power distance
Large .... Small

Power of the group
Individualistic .... Group-oriented

Uncertainty avoidance
Low .... High

Assertiveness
Masculine .... Feminine

Orientation to life
Long-term .... Short-term

C. COMMUNICATION STYLES

Context

Low .... High

Verbal styles

Direct .... Indirect
Linear .... Circular
Informal .... Formal
Confrontational .... Compliant
Initiating .... Listening
Factual .... Intuitive
Rational .... Emotive

Nonverbal styles

Vocalics *(e.g., accents, pitch, and volume)*
Tone of voice: *Harsh* .... *Soft*
Eye contact:　*Maintain* ....*Break off* .... *Avert*
Touching:　　*Bow* ....*Handshake* .... *Continual*

D. SENSE OF PERSONAL PHYSICAL SPACE

Distant .... Close

E. SENSE OF TIME

Monochronic .... Polychronic

Chapter 6

THE SELF IN RELATION TO OTHERS

Now that we have described the self as a cultural self and looked at our cultural variabilities, we move to describing groups in society. As humans, we are social people. We tend to interact in groups.

The groups we belong to, such as family, school, church, work, community, and society, give us a sense of identity. Who we are is defined by the groups to which we belong.

Groups that you belong to are called your *in-groups*.

Groups that you do not belong to are called your *out-groups*.

Look back at the cultural groups listed on pages 39–40. For each group, name your in-group and your out-group(s).

For example, with regard to socioeconomic status, those in the blue-collar working class tend to socialize together (in-group), while those from the white-collar professional class tend to socialize together (in-group). For each, the other is their out-group.

There is a tendency for us to see members of our in-groups more favorably than members of our out-groups.

As the saying goes, birds of a feather flock together.

We also tend to consider members of an out-group to be generally alike, while we see many distinguishing characteristics among members of our in-groups. Because we spend more time with our in-group members, we see and experience their differences.

For example, within the female cultural group, women see many subgroups with differing value sets. Some men, however, might say that all women are the same. A few examples of female subgroups include: women who are sports oriented and those who are not; women who wear makeup and jewelry and those who do not; women who see the man as boss and those who do not. What other examples can you think of?

Because we tend to favor in-group members, we have less contact with members of our out-group(s).

We have a tendency to trust and be more loyal to in-group members and to exclude out-group members. Within the in-group, loyalty and trust tend to be reciprocal. I trust you and you trust me simply because we are members of the same in-group. We do not necessarily need a personal relationship with all in-group members. We just *know* we can trust each other.

In-group/out-
group relation-
ships become
more complex when we think
of the many groups that we belong
to at any given time.

Thus, you might be part of my in-group for
race, but belong to my out-group for socioeconomic status.

Taken together, all of your in-groups make up
your social identity. Each person identifies
more with some groups than with others. For
example, a European-American woman might
not identify strongly with the European-
American group, while having a strong connection to her gender group.

In-groups vary with the context and the situation. For example, students in a high-school class are considered an in-group, and students in a different class are their out-group.

If both classes go on a field trip with students from other schools, however, the two classes feel more like one in-group. The students feel more loyal to all of the students from their own school than to the students from other schools.

Thus, how much we feel connected to a member of an in-group might vary with the situation.

If we tend to exclude individuals in our out-groups, regard them as generally alike, and feel less trust for them than we do for in-group members, we are less likely to gain an understanding of them and their lives.

To build a more inclusive community, we must become aware of our in-group/out-group biases and be open to learning more about out-group members.

We do this by practicing the skills of mindfulness, listening with empathy, and mindful interpretation. When we apply these skills, we avoid labeling out-group members unfavorably and become more open to the way they see the world. Section Four, The Evolving Skill Set, discusses these skills in more depth.

Now, let's look at the in-group/out-group perspective within the context of organizations and institutions. Who are the in-groups in society? Who makes the rules that build our organizations and institutions?

In-groups and Out-groups in the United States

To understand the in-group/out-group phenomenon in the United States, we must go
back to the people who made the rules when
this country was founded. From a cultural perspective, these founders were white, male,
Christian landowners. There were no women,
people of color, nonlandowners, or non-
Christians in the original decision-making
group.

What to do with those whom
society cannot accommodate?
Criminalize them. Outlaw
their actions and creations.
Declare them the enemy....
Gangs are not alien powers.
They begin as unstructured
groupings, our children, who
desire the same as any young
person. Respect. A sense of
belonging. Protection. The
same thing that the YMCA,
Little League or the Boy
Scouts want.

Luis J. Rodriguez
Always Running:
La Vida Loca, Gang Days in L.A.

This group laid the foundation for a nation based on their common value system. While their words were magnifi-cent—"All men are created equal"—their frame of reference was their own cultural world-view. They saw the world through their own cultural lenses.

If women had been the country's founders, and if men had been excluded from property ownership and decision-making, the words may have been "All women are created equal." Men, then, may have been taught that the word "women" meant men, too.

Long ago in the United States basic decisions were made. The most important of these made color the crucial variable. This began as the cornerstone of the system of black slavery. After refinements, it has remained to become imbedded in the national character. Persisting to this day is an attitude, shared by black and white alike, that blacks are inferior.

Price Cobbs and William Grier
Black Rage

In-groups that hold rule-making power tend to hold on to that power. In the United States today, this power and authority remains largely in the hands of the same cultural in-groups as those who founded the nation. The situation is perpetuated by the diffusion of the founders' values, beliefs, and norms throughout society, which limited the power of out-groups.

The justification for slavery was the assumption that black people were inferior and sub-human. The belief that they were "less" than whites was so deeply diffused throughout society that many blacks believed it, too.

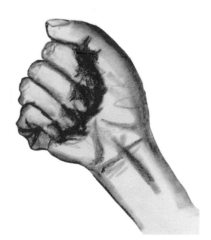

Whites simply don't
know that the rules
that work for them may
not work at all for black
men.

Price Cobbs and William Grier
The Jesus Bag

This quote bothers me as an
African-American. I have
been taught that there is a
hidden agenda, and that
whites are quite aware that
the rules do not work for
people of color. That is why
the rules are constantly
changing to continue to keep
us in the dark so we can't get
ahead. It's the power and
control that keep oppression
alive and well.

Pamala Morris
Purdue University

Here we see two opposing views from African-American
professionals. They are seeds for dialogue about the perceptions, attitudes, and assumptions in our society today.

The belief that blacks are not equal to whites still exists, sometimes openly, as in the white supremacy movement, but often more covertly, through subtle actions that reflect underlying attitudes, assumptions, and perceptions, based on nonacceptance of differences.

These subtle actions sometimes are more destructive than the more open actions of white supremacists. They are like the tiny, biting gnats known as "no-see-ums." You feel the discrimination, but you cannot see it coming and thus cannot avoid it. You do react, however, and sometimes the reaction is harmful to your sense of self.

In the United States, our major institutions and organizations reflect the norms, values, and beliefs of the dominant culture.

For example, our organizations generally operate from the dominant cultural value of "Time is money." We also value independent work and workers who are efficient, effective, and can accomplish a lot.

Some nondominant cultural groups value time as the only resource we are sure we have. Honoring relationships with others is more important than being on time. In Native American and Latino-American cultures, when a relative dies, attending the ceremony in honor of his life is more important than work. It may make no difference how close the relative is or whether there are pressures and deadlines at work.

Organizations that operate from dominant cultural values often have limited tolerance for this "time" away from work.

This simple example of the in-group (dominant culture) making the rules to the exclusion of out-groups demonstrates how deeply rooted culture is and how slowly it changes. For each of the 14 cultural dimensions described in Chapter 2, try thinking about how the in-group/out-group effect has manifested itself in society.

Our challenge today is to become aware of how these systems do not serve the needs of some cultural groups. With awareness of cultural differences, we can begin to work with others to build institutions and organizations that are more flexible and inclusive. When we do, we will uncover a richness of human talent just waiting to be shared.

Summary

As social beings with a culture, we belong to groups. We have closer ties to some groups than to others. The groups we belong to are our in-groups. All others are our out-groups. We trust our own in-group members and tend to exclude those who are not part of our group. By doing so, we keep our lives in order and our identities intact. It feels safer to stay in our own group.

At the U.S. societal level, certain in-groups established a system of rules and excluded their out-groups. Draw-ing on their own cultural mind set, they set up a system that gave their in-groups the advantage. They held decision-making power and have passed those advantages and deci-sion-making powers down through the generations to their own in-group members.

While acknowledging all that has gone before us, it is our responsi-bility to recreate our systems in ways that truly honor the belief that all of us are created equal.

Chapter 7

THE POWER DYNAMIC

As people who care about creating an environment in which everyone is accepted, respected, and honored for their gifts and talents, we must see and understand the power dynamic played out in our intercultural relationships.

Power is closely related to the in-group/out-group phenomenon described in the previous chapter. Power issues are always present but rarely are acknowledged openly.

What is power? Borrowing from Broom and Klein, *power is energy in use*. From the perspective of physics, power is a force in movement to make something happen. The *American Heritage Dictionary* says that power is the exertion of strength or force as well as the ability or capacity to perform effectively. Thus, power is a force that affects an outcome.

The contributions that women and people of color would make if invited to participate fully with men and whites in the game of power would certainly be remarkable. Moreover, the mutual learning produced by this perceptual shift would act as a vital key unlocking the harmonic potential of technologies, organizations, societies, and perhaps the entire world.

Michael Broom and Don Klein
Power: The Infinite Game

We all have power and have felt the effects of power. We exercise power over ourselves as well as in relation to others.

Thus, power is manifested at three levels:

- self

- group

- society

Power within the self is reflected in our thoughts and in our internal self-talk.

Our actions demonstrate our sense of power. Power in the group can include dynamics in families, organizations, and workplaces. Power in society is manifested through rules and norms at the community, regional, and national level.

Power is experienced in various dimensions:

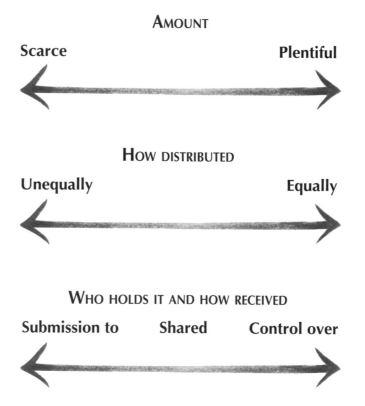

AMOUNT

Scarce   **Plentiful**

HOW DISTRIBUTED

Unequally   **Equally**

WHO HOLDS IT AND HOW RECEIVED

Submission to   **Shared**   **Control over**

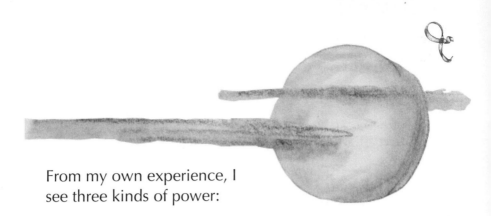

From my own experience, I
see three kinds of power:

- *personal power:* our capacity to exert our
  energy toward our own outcomes

- *influential power:* our capacity to influence outcomes

- *decision-making power:* our capacity to
  decide outcomes

Each one varies within the three power
dimensions just described.

In relationships of perma-
nent inequality, power
cements dominance and
subordination, and oppression is rationalized by
theories that "explain" the
need for its continuation.

Carol Gilligan
*In a Different Voice: Psychological
Theory and Women's Development*

PERSONAL POWER

Personal power is our capacity to exert our energy toward a certain outcome.

I can be/do   **I cannot be/do**

While there are those who exercise their personal power continually, others have abundant personal power but are unaware of it because they have not learned how to use it. Thus, it lies dormant. Some believe they have no power. If we are aware of our personal power, we can use it for personal success as well as for outcomes that affect others.

Personal power is affected by the outside influences of one's groups and society, and it can vary by circumstance.

While personal power is primarily concerned with perceptions of the self, influential and decision-making power is concerned with the self as it is perceived by others. Others, here, refers to the family, group, community, or society as a whole.

Many years earlier I, or
rather someone very like me
and certainly related to me,
had been taken from Africa
by force. This second-leave-
taking would not be so
onerous, for now I knew my
people had never completely
left Africa. We had sung it
in our blues, shouted it in
our gospel and danced the
continent in our breakdowns.

Maya Angelou
All God's Children Need Traveling Shoes

INFLUENTIAL POWER

Influential power is our capacity to exert our energy to influence a desired outcome within our own groups and/or society.

Great influence   **No influence**

Situational influence

Where we fall on this continuum varies with regard to the groups we belong to and our role in society. For example, at work I might be able to influence how we work as a team, but in society, my influence might be limited to working on an election campaign and casting my vote.

Situational influence refers to how power to affect an outcome varies with the specific situation and with time. For example, as a new member of a group I may have little influential power, but as group members get to know me and listen to my ideas, my influential power may increase.

In situations where we do not have decision-making power, our knowledge, persuasion skills, and relationship with decision-makers allow us to use our influential power to affect decisions.

DECISION-MAKING POWER

Decision-making power is our capacity to exert our energy toward deciding outcomes.

Great power   **No power**

Situational decision-making power

Again, decision-making power varies as it relates to self, group, and society. We may have decision-making power with regard to self and groups in which we have authority. Decision-making power within our in-groups may depend on the situation. Voting power or charitable-giving power may be the forms of decision-making power we have in the community.

It also is possible that decisions with regard to self influence decisions within our in-groups and within society. For example, if a professional office worker decides to treat a janitor with dignity and respect, others might see the effects of that decision and do the same.

In a group, personal, influential, and decision-making power are dynamic. For example, an adolescent son might want to take a group of friends on a long road trip (desire to use personal power). His older sister explains why this is not a good idea and suggests they take the train instead (influential power). His parent says he cannot have a car to take the road trip (decision-making power). The son then decides, with the permission of his family, to go on vacation with his best friend's family (individual, influential, and decision-making power intertwined).

From the societal perspective, many cultural groups do not have influential or decision-making power. When society denies power to certain groups, the individuals in these power-less groups begin to limit their own personal power. One aspect of the black movement in the United States has been to enable black people to regain personal power. Greater personal power in turn points the way toward sharing in influential and decision-making powers in society.

As we work with difference in communities, it is essential to be aware of the power dynamic at play. This power dynamic can affect whether or not a person is respected and honored for the gifts he or she brings to a setting.

We can use our personal power to effect change toward more inclusive communities. Deciding to use our personal power to create more inclusive communities originates in our heart set.

Section Three

THE OPEN HEART SET

Chapter 8   About Commitment and Caring

There can be no knowledge
without emotion. We may
be aware of a truth, yet
until we have felt its force,
it is not ours. To the
cognition of the brain we
must add the experience of
the soul.

Arnold Bennett

Chapter 8

ABOUT COMMITMENT AND CARING

An open heart set is interconnected with an inquiring mind set and an evolving skill set. The mind set refers to how we think about difference, and the skill set is what we do when faced with difference. The heart set is how we feel about developing and practicing our mind set and skill set.

The heart set shines light on our commitment and willingness to work with people who are different from ourselves. It is about caring enough to create environments where all voices are heard and respected. If we do not have an open heart set, the mind and skill sets become irrelevant. Thus, an open heart set is the key to working with differences.

If you have read this far, you probably already have an open heart set!

An open heart set involves being with others:

- with care

- with respect

- with curiosity

- without judgment

It is as if you were holding another person in the palm of your hand with gentleness and care.

An open heart set involves a commitment to:

- honor others while honoring yourself

- continue to learn about yourself and others

- stay in communication even when it becomes difficult

- call on your inquiring mind set and evolving skill set to guide you and others to mutual understanding

An open heart set involves a willingness to:

- pay attention to your own inner feelings and messages

- reflect on those feelings and messages as a way to enhance your cultural self-awareness

I want to appreciate you
without judging

Join you
without invading

Invite you
without demanding

Leave you without guilt.

Virginia Satir
Making Contact

Sometimes, when interacting with another person, the differences are so great that we feel a thick wall go up between us. We judge and we feel that the other person is wrong. The easy road is to close the heart and end the communication.

When the wall goes up, and negative judgment sets in, work from an open heart set perspective. Here are seven ways of an open heart set:

- Take time to reflect and listen to your inner feelings.

- Acknowledge that there might be more to see in the interaction than you now see. Feel your openness or resistance to this acknowledgment.

- Consider that there might be a difference between what the other person **meant** and what you **understood**. Feel how open or closed you are to this possibility.

- Become clear about your common goal and your desired common outcome. Listen to your feelings about your power to work toward the common outcome.

- Imagine the other as a caring person who wants the best outcome for this situation.

- Feel the synergy created by dialogue in which you learn from each other and explore creative possibilities for an outcome that honors you both.

- Sometimes it helps to take some time away from the situation. When you feel ready, go back to the person and try again to communicate toward mutual understanding.

When taking a break from a conflict situation, you might find it helpful to:

- take time to play

- laugh and be silly

- be creative

Laughter and play are restorative.

So is contemplative time alone.

An open heart set involves taking care of yourself so that you can be caring with others.

Try this:

Draw four straight lines that connect all nine dots without lifting your pencil from the paper. It is possible!

●   ●   ●

●   ●   ●

●   ●   ●

(Answer at the end of this chapter)

Being creative helps you see outside your box, that is, your own perspective. It creates an attitude that allows you to do what you previously thought was impossible.

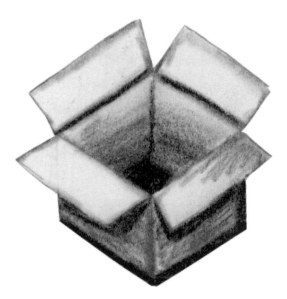

Remember: when we encounter difference, the potential learning cycle looks like this:

- First we don't know that we don't know—until an intercultural event fails.

- Then, we know that we don't know. We are aware that we need to learn more, and we begin.

- Soon, we don't know that we know. We begin to integrate new knowledge and skills into our own communication style.

- And then, we know that we know. We make these skills a conscious part of our interactions.

- And then the learning cycle starts over— something we've never encountered before occurs....

An open heart set includes a readiness to **listen** to others. The Chinese character Ting (Listen) incorporates all of the elements of good listening: ear, eye, mind, and heart. Learning to listen attentively on all of these levels is central to working with differences.

Ting Listen

Ear

Mind

Eye

Heart

ESSENCE OF AN OPEN HEART SET

When I begin to see myself as a person framed by my culture, I become aware of layers of learning that have told me what to see, what to believe, and what is right.

As I begin to bring those parts of myself to conscious awareness, I can decide which parts I want to keep and which parts I want to change. I must accept and believe in myself as the best person I can be at the moment, while continually changing and improving.

At the same time, I am learning that others have different cultures. There are many layers to another person's culture, just as there are to my own. Now I begin to look at others through my "cultural awareness" glasses and marvel at the differences among us.

I become someone who is curious and wants to learn about differences. I no longer judge others to be right or wrong as quickly as I did before. Instead I learn to value what each person brings to the community. Through this openness, I become more accepting and respectful of others.

THE NINE-DOT EXERCISE

on page 184

ONE POSSIBLE ANSWER

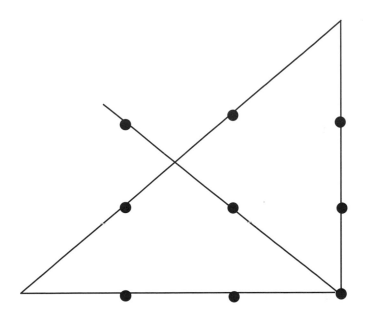

Only when we are willing to think outside of the box are we able to figure out how to complete this exercise according to the instructions. We have been conditioned through our cultural upbringing to stay inside the lines when we think of solving this problem. How does this exercise apply to developing intercultural competence?

To recognize or admit differ-
ences, even among the species
of life, does not require then
that human beings create
forces to forge to gain a sense
of unity or homogeneity. To
exist in a creation means that
living is more than tolerance
for other life forms—it is
recognition that in differences
there is the strength of cre-
ation and that this strength is
a deliberate desire of the
creator.

Vine Deloria, Jr.
God Is Red: A Native View of Religion

Section Four

THE EVOLVING SKILL SET

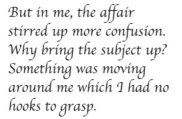

But in me, the affair
stirred up more confusion.
Why bring the subject up?
Something was moving
around me which I had no
hooks to grasp.

Zora Neale Hurston
Dust Tracks on the Road

Chapter 9

DEVELOPING YOUR INTERCULTURAL SKILL SET

Now that you have added to your mind set and have a commitment to your heart set, you can begin to apply these two sets to the development of a skill set. In this chapter, I describe nine intercultural skills that you can begin to practice as you go about your daily interactions.

Intentionally practicing these nine skills requires your whole body to pay attention—both when interacting with others and when reflecting on your internal reactions, both physical and mental. The stronger your physical reaction—coupled with a negative mental reaction—the greater the difference between yourself and the other person. As difficult as it is to admit, within this interaction lies a grand opportunity for learning.

How can I develop the skills to learn from others?

How can I stay open, curious, and nonjudgmental when another's communication style makes me uncomfortable?

Perhaps the best way is to practice the following skills one at a time with a trusted friend who will give you honest feedback to support your learning.

Whether you practice with a partner or alone, you can begin to develop these nine specific skills:

- mindfulness

- observation

- listening to your internal messages

- listening with empathy

- mindful interpretation

- giving feedback

- acknowledging failure

- acknowledging "not knowing"

- mutual adaptation

MINDFULNESS

Often connected with Eastern thought, mindfulness is about paying close attention to your inner self. From an Eastern perspective, one begins to develop mindfulness by focusing on breathing and meditation.

Social psychologist Ellen Langer has taken a Western look at mindfulness. I find Langer's work to be very helpful in developing mindfulness as a skill for Western minds.

To understand mindfulness, I begin with its opposite, mindlessness. I remember the day my mother found her dishcloth in the refrigerator. It scared her. She had no idea how it got there, but she knew she must have put it there. Putting the dishcloth in the refrigerator with no awareness of the action is an example of mindless behavior.

We all have mindless behaviors. The most common example is breathing. I breathe all day and rarely am aware of it. Other examples include tying my shoes, brushing my teeth, and typing a letter. My mind often is somewhere else when I am involved in these activities. When I am typing, I do not think about where each key is. I think of the ideas I want to convey. If I stopped to ask myself where the letter "q" is, for example, I would lose my rhythm. I just know where each letter is because I have practiced typing for many years.

Mindless behavior results from repetition or a familiar situation that lets us become mentally lazy. We form a mind set when we first encounter something, and we see it the same way when we encounter it again. When we are mindless, our mind is set in a certain way before we think or reflect. Have you ever bumped into a store mannequin and said "Excuse me"?

Seeing things only one way traps us, and we act from a single perspective. When we do so, we are limited. We see only what we expect to see, when, in fact, there might be much more. We have unknowingly filtered out other possibilities.

Mindfulness, on the other hand, is more playful. It involves:

- continually finding new ways to describe something

- openness to new information

- awareness of more than one perspective

When we are open to new information, find new ways to describe what we see, and try different perspectives, we gain more options for responding to a situation. We open ourselves to becoming empathetic with others. We see the possibility of choosing from two or more alternatives.

Developing mindfulness

Practice describing and redescribing

To begin, try this exercise. Find a pen or a paper clip. List everything these objects can be besides what you automatically think they are.

Next, go into a public place and observe others. Imagine what might be true about them in addition to what you first see. For example, in addition to seeing a sloppily dressed person, see someone who stayed up all night to help a sick friend, or someone who just completed his first novel, or someone without access to laundry facilities. Be as creative as possible. Notice the energy and positive outlook you are building.

Welcome new information and other points of view

When discussing a problem or situation, ask for other viewpoints. Try asking for a viewpoint opposite the one currently being presented. Try to come up with as many viewpoints as possible.

One way to develop this skill is to take a walk in a forest or park when the trees are in leaf. How many shades of green can you see? Keep looking for new shades. When you look for new information, you often find much more than you expected.

Be open to more than one right view

There can be as many different views as there are observers. When you say another view can be right, you become open to greater understanding. The next time you are involved in a discussion, say to yourself, "That view is valid. It is right from this other person's perspective." Try adopting the other's perspective for a moment. Sit with it. Imagine the perspective as valid rather than invalid.

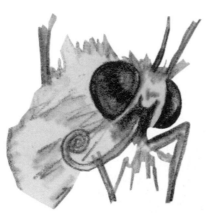

Mindfulness encourages intuition and creativity, while also allowing us to think and analyze. By doing so, we gain understanding and new insights.

Mindlessness maintains assumptions about the status quo. Those who benefit from a narrow view resist other views that feel like a threat to their security. Mindfulness leads to the discovery of new possibilities beyond the status quo.

OBSERVATION

In trying to make sense of what we see and hear, we often automatically jump to quick conclusions. Along with being mindful in our interactions with one another, we need the ability to take in information in a way that allows us to change our mind about our interpretations of what we see.

Try this exercise.

What do you see in this picture? Write down your answer.

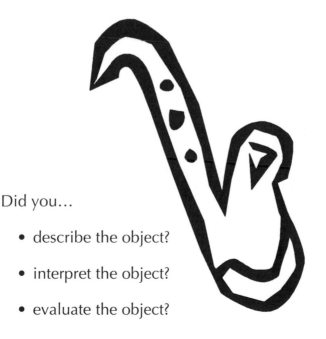

Did you...

- describe the object?

- interpret the object?

- evaluate the object?

The following are examples of each of these ways to view the object on the previous page:

Describing—The object is a black-and-white drawing with thick lines and is about 3 inches long. The lines are curved, coming together in a sharp downward point at the top. There are three dots in the top center of the shape.

Interpreting—This is a bird. The bird is wearing a bib and has a long tail that has three dots on it.

Evaluating—This is a poorly drawn saxophone.

Often, interpreting and evaluating are easier than describing. Describing requires careful observation, while interpreting and evaluating flow naturally from our personal perspectives.

Often, we think we are describing what we see, when in fact we are ascribing a meaning to it. We are interpreting it and/or judging it, evaluating its worth.

To observe without immediately interpreting or evaluating is a learned skill.

One way to practice observation without quick judgment is to begin by describing what you see. For example, when you see a young person walking down the street, rather than saying, "There goes an obnoxious teenager," describe what you see. Open yourself to new perspectives. You might see the teenager as someone who walks with a fast pace, holds his head down, and steps out of the way to allow a mother with a baby in a stroller to pass by.

As you encounter others, work on observing and describing before interpreting. After awhile, observing first and suspending judgment becomes natural. You stay open, curious, and engaged in possibility.

LISTENING TO YOUR INTERNAL MESSAGES

When interacting with someone who is culturally different, paying attention to our internal physical reaction is a key skill. Sometimes, we ignore our physical signals and attempt to stay in control. That is when we react from our most ethnocentric state.

Our bodies can be like a lighthouse that warns us to pay attention. To do so, we must know our own capabilities and have maps (mind–heart–skill sets) to guide us through the challenging waters.

For example, I have learned that African-Americans, as well as many other groups of color, have developed an adaptive communication technique called buffering. Because African-Americans have experienced countless messages that they are not worthwhile (e.g., "You don't belong in this town"), they have developed buffers to keep negative messages from wounding their sense of self-worth. Buffers are like an invisible shield that keeps the emotional content of negative messages from penetrating the psyche. To a non-African-American, African-Americans might seem to be on guard.

When I sense that an African-American is on guard, knowing about buffering makes it easier to listen with empathy. I am aware that this person has developed buffers to keep safe in a white-ruled society.

Empathy is different from feeling sorry for someone or feeling guilty about injustice associated with someone's race or gender. It simply means acknowledging another person's reality and being open to his or her perspective.

The best way to practice listening skills is to not talk—to remain silent and be attentive. Then paraphrase the verbal and nonverbal message and feelings you heard to make sure you understood. Remaining silent takes a conscious effort for those of us who like to fill the empty airtime with words. Practice focusing on understanding the other person's reality instead of getting your point across.

MINDFUL INTERPRETATION

In trying to make sense of our interactions, we tend to judge others based on our own values and beliefs. To interpret mindfully means to become aware of our thought patterns that lead to this judgment as well as our verbal and nonverbal reactions. Next, we suspend our final judgment and take time to draw on our mind set, listen with empathy, and provide feedback.

Mindful interpretation simply means to be aware of our internal processing and to apply our intercultural knowledge and skills to expand the possibilities of understanding the interaction.

We still interpret meaning from messages we receive, but we do so with more awareness of the process. We stay open to new information that might change our mind.

GIVING FEEDBACK

Once we have listened with empathy, observed with curiosity, and interpreted with mindfulness, we need to check whether we understand the other person's intended meaning. We can do so by:

- Paraphrasing what we understood. This usually causes the speaker to say more and often brings more clarity. Another method is to say, "Is this what you mean...?" (In a neutral tone describe what you understood was said.)

- Do not be discouraged if it turns out that you have misunderstood. It is far better that you know it! You are getting closer to understanding the intended meaning in the message.

- If you do not understand, you can say, "I don't understand, please tell me more," in a curious, interested tone.

- You also can verbalize the feelings and tone that you sense. "My sense is that you are angry about this...."

- Giving feedback also includes acknowledgment by saying "Yes" or "I see."

- The next step to feedback is to acknowledge your own reactions. This step is necessary if you want to reach "mutual adaptation," that is, a mutually defined solution to your dilemma.

- I acknowledge my reactions in a nonblaming way: "I understand how you see this situation. Interestingly, I see it in a completely different way...." (Then, I describe my perspective.) Another example is: "I'm aware that we come from two very different cultures. I feel awkward about how to greet you when I come into the room. How do you like to be greeted?"

An intercultural conversation is most effective when we take time to check for understanding of the intended communication. Ongoing feedback is an essential part of checking for meaning.

ACKNOWLEDGING FAILURE

Because effective intercultural communication is so challenging, there are bound to be times when an interaction fails. Recognizing the failure and not blaming yourself or the other person is key. One way to acknowledge that the communication has failed and that you still want to understand is to apologize: "I don't think that worked. I'm sorry. Can we try again?"

ACKNOWLEDGING "NOT KNOWING"

When working with difference, there are times when we just don't "get it." This is the fuzzy state of ambiguity when meaning is not clear. Acknowledge that this state of "not knowing" is part of moving toward deeper understanding.

"Not knowing" is like being stuck in a vat of molasses. You can move through it, but only very slowly, with time and patience. "Not knowing" is an OK place to be. Sometimes we have to be in a state of "not knowing" for awhile.

MUTUAL ADAPTATION

In many conversations with those who are culturally different from yourself, you will find differing communication and decision-making styles and/or perspectives.

Mutual adaptation is about each person being open to adapting his or her style and decision-making process to the other person's. Each person is respected and validated.

When a decision affects both of you, together you decide the best course of action through empathetic listening. The decision that emerges will be right for the specific context and situation. (You might want to look back at the five-stage developmental learning process on pages 60–62.)

A simple example of mutual adaptation occurs when I greet my Latino friends. Latino acquaintances usually greet one another with an embrace and a kiss on the cheek. Anglo friends might hug but more often simply greet one another verbally.

When an Anglo and Latino become friends, the internal dialogue begins. Do I hug or not? What about the kiss on the cheek?

Through a series of nonverbal cues, we carefully observe each other to determine the most respectful greeting ritual. It might be just the hug and not the kiss, or it might be simply touching each other's arm.

In all cases, it is a mutual adaptation to each other's styles. This adaptive decision unfolds in less time than it takes to read about it.

You can only practice the skill of mutual adaptation with others. It involves careful listening to understand the other's reality and preferred decision. For mutual adaptation to occur, both parties use the intercultural communication guidelines listed in the next chapter.

Mutual adaptation requires time to develop trust and time to listen and understand one another. It is the greatest intercultural skill I know of and one that brings new possibilities for resolving previously unsolvable problems. It is a way of honoring and respecting one another of the highest order. It is a win–win situation. Power is shared equally, and new power is created.

SUMMARY

These nine skills...

- mindfulness

- observation

- listening to your internal messages

- listening with empathy

- mindful interpretation

- giving feedback

- acknowledging failure

- acknowledging "not knowing"

- mutual adaptation

...when practiced, become an art. This art continually creates new possibilities. You can develop these skills only through daily practice. At first, the skills might seem impossible to develop, but with time and repetition they become easier.

The next chapter applies the skills described in this chapter to an intercultural interaction.

Chapter 10

APPLYING YOUR INTERCULTURAL SKILL SET

This chapter integrates your new skill set into a set of guidelines for intercultural communication. To truly understand, you must lift these words from the page, take them into your own life, and make them come alive through practice.

Focus on one guideline at a time. Once you have mastered it and incorporated it into your daily practice, move on to the next.

At first, this process is like learning to ride a bike. You feel wobbly and unsure, and you may fall. This is all part of learning. The more you practice following these guidelines, the quicker you will master them. Eventually all of these guidelines will become part of how you communicate with others. They then will seem easy.

The more I study and experience, the more I believe that almost everyone I meet can be considered a "culturally different other." Of course, some are more different from me than others.

For example, in the midst of an intense conflict, I finally perceived my partner as a person whose culture is different from mine. He is a white male who was raised in an educated, upper-middle-class, Midwestern home, and he has a "being-in-the-present" outlook. I am a white female, raised in a blue-collar to white-collar middle-class home on the East Coast, and I live in a "let's-get-it-done" mode.

Once I began to see these differences as cultural, I began to shift negative judgments and became more open to learning how to see and feel his perspective. In other words, I began to empathize with and validate his worldview.

I have professional colleagues and friends who are African-American, Native American, European-American, Chinese-American, and Latino. I also have gay, lesbian, and bisexual friends and colleagues. The degree of difference varies with each of them, but in every case there are value and communication style differences related to race, ethnicity, national origin, or sexual orientation. At the same time, there might be cultural similarities related to gender, age, education, or profession.

In all cases, I apply the same skills (from Chapter 9) and the guidelines presented in this chapter. It takes energy, practice, and awareness to do so effectively. The results, however, make the effort worthwhile. My life has become much richer and filled with new insights and adventures as a result.

I also have walked away from some encounters shaking my head about how poorly I applied my skills. I learn from my mistakes, work on forgiving myself for my limits, and move on.

Whenever I interact with someone who is different from myself (that is, just about everyone), I try to keep the following guidelines in mind:

- **Be open**—Approach each interaction with a "culturally different other" mindful of any assumptions, attitudes, or perceptions that would filter out the other's message. I try to be aware of these filters and recognize that they might affect the interaction. Then, I consciously attempt to set these thoughts aside so that I can be open to experiencing more than I expected.

  For example, if I value heterosexuality as normal and am talking with someone who is gay, I might limit my perception and only see this person as a sexual being. Thus, I filter out the fact that he or she is a great writer, a wonderful listener, and has a kind heart. Being open means to become aware of my assumptions, which are evident in internal self-talk, and to hold the assumptions in check. Then, I can begin to see the gifts and talents this person has to offer.

- **Keep my mind set ready** to help me understand the interaction. I make the information in Section Two of this book a part of my mental knowledge bank. Then, I can recognize each interaction as fitting into certain verbal or nonverbal communication patterns. This helps me interpret the true meaning of the other person's message. It also keeps me curious.

- **Stay curious**—Staying curious keeps me from making judgments too quickly. I say to myself, "There is more to learn in this interaction than I already know. What is it?" I remain curious by being open and using my knowledge as I listen.

- **Be accepting and inquisitive**—Even if I don't agree, I listen to understand what is being said. I accept what is being said as the other's valid experience. I stay open to find out what the speaker means.

- **Listen, listen, listen** while drawing on the mind set to understand. Listening requires complete attention to both words and nonverbal cues. It also requires that I pay attention to my own inner responses, both "feelings in the gut" and thoughts. These inner responses help me shape my clarifying questions.

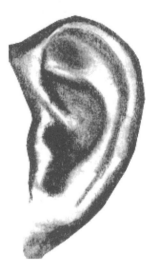

- **Ask clarifying questions** to understand the real meaning. A clarifying question is a nonjudgmental question that helps me learn what the speaker really intends to communicate. Sometimes the question is about what is being said. Sometimes, it is about feelings that are being communicated. Examples of clarifying questions include:

    Tell me more about....

    I'm not sure I understand. Is what you are saying...?

    What is a ...?

    My sense is that you are feeling.... Is this true?

Although "why" questions are my favorite kind of question, I have found that they are **not** useful in clarifying a situation. "Why" questions make people defensive and do not lead to greater understanding. "What" questions seem more effective at increasing understanding.

- **Feel what is being communicated**—For communication to be effective, I must empathize with the speaker. Not only must I interpret the facts of the message, but I also must understand the feelings behind the message. Mentally naming the feelings I perceive helps me clarify the feelings contained in the message. I then can ask a clarifying question, "My sense is that you are feeling…. Is this so?"

- **Validate what is being communicated** with a nod, an attentive expression, a verbal response such as "I see" or "Never thought of that" or "Interesting." In this way I acknowledge what the person is communicating. Validation does not necessarily mean I agree, but simply that "I hear you." Validating what a person says also validates the speaker.

- **Say what I want to say without blaming the other**—When I respond, I must frame my words to reflect what I am feeling and thinking in a way that does not imply judgment. This is tricky because it is easier for me to interpret situations in a way that makes me right, which might make the other wrong. I must neutralize my response so that we both can stay open to continual learning. One way to do this is to shift my response from "You feel or do this…" to "When I listen to you, I feel and do… because I am…."

- **Use nonverbal cues that are open, inclusive, and receiving** yet adaptive to the person I am with. Using my mind set, I observe others' nonverbal cues as well as my own. I use nonverbals that communicate that I am not in a hurry, that I am interested in the conversation, and that I am showing respect. I become aware of the tone of my voice.

- **Continue the dialogue and, when ready, bring it to closure** by acknowledging the other person and the value of the experience. Bringing an interaction to closure is a very important way to honor what just happened. The interaction becomes complete for that moment.

This is a long list of things to do all at once in an interaction. The interaction is easier if the other person has the same skill set. Then, the communication becomes one of mutual respect, understanding, and adaptation.

What happens if the other doesn't have the same skill set? In that case, I still practice the skills, but I must work harder at adapting my style to the other's style. It is my responsibility to adapt, since I have the knowledge and capability to do so. By adapting to the other, I validate the other's experience and show respect. It is my way of code-shifting to ensure as positive an outcome as possible.

What if we try too hard to make the conversation work? If both people have intercultural communication skills, each tends to adapt to the other's style. Once, while talking with a Native American scholar, I noticed that he was averting his eyes. I am aware that Native Americans tend to avert their eyes when talking with someone they respect, so I began to avert my eyes. I wanted to show him respect. I was trying to adapt. At the same time, he began to use more direct eye contact with me. He was trying to adapt to my style as well.

It became an unspoken eye dance between us. The message that we communicated, however, was one of mutual respect. Through this awkward adaptation, the intent was clear and appreciated.

Some intercultural interactions go well, and some don't. Learn from each one. Appreciate yourself for making the effort and for practicing your intercultural communication skills. Mentally note what went well and what you would change. Be clear about your intentions and, when ready, move on to your next interaction.

INTERCULTURAL INTERACTION GUIDELINES
AT A GLANCE

Below is a list of these 12 guidelines. Refer to it as you practice your evolving skill set.

- Be open.

- Keep your mind set ready.

- Stay curious.

- Be accepting and inquisitive.

- Listen, listen, listen.

- Ask clarifying questions.

- Be authentic in the experience.

- Feel what is being communicated.

- Validate what is being communicated.

- Say what you want to say without blaming the other.

- Use nonverbal cues that are open, inclusive, and receiving.

- Continue the dialogue and, when ready, bring it to closure.

Chapter 11

LISTENING TO THE VOICES OF OTHERS

When we listen to the stories of those from other cultures, we share in their experiences and increase our awareness of differences. We begin to realize that our experience of reality or our culture's "right way" is only one of many.

In this chapter, you'll find 12 stories from individuals who have been brave enough to share one of their life's stories. They ask only to be accepted as they are. These are their stories of personal truth—truths that might be very different from your own. These stories provide an opportunity to practice the intercultural skills and guidelines outlined in Chapters 9 and 10.

On n'a voit bien qu'avec le
coeur, l'essential est invisible
pour les yeux.

(One only sees truly with the
heart, what is essential is
invisible to the eye.)

Antoine de Saint-Exupéry
Le Petit Prince
(The Little Prince)

Some of these stories might make you uncomfortable. They are opportunities to practice "listening" without judgment. If you feel yourself reacting negatively to any part of them, you might want to take a break and read them later. In the meantime, review the mind set and skill set sections of this book.

Look for examples of value sets, communication styles, power dynamics, and in-group/out-group dynamics in these stories. Reading these stories can deepen your understanding of the mind, heart, and skill sets.

These stories revolve around several core dimensions of diversity: race, ethnicity, age, gender, sexual orientation, and physical abilities. They reflect experiences of being outside the dominant U.S. culture as well as experiences of being part of the dominant U.S. culture. Each story tells of an experience with difference.

THE STORIES

El Norte (The North)—Mario Magaña
   Crossing the U.S.–Mexican border to make
   a new life

From Hawaii to Oregon—Sharon Takahashi
   A Japanese-American's perspective

Going Shopping—Pamala Morris
   An African-American visiting a small town

Where Are YOU from?—Sarah Harrison
   A weekly challenge to one's sense of
   belonging

I Decided to Wear African—Ken Grimes
   Being different means always being a
   teacher

The Beauty of Difference—Steve Hanamura
   Living with a physical limitation, blind from
   birth

The Effect of Spanish as My First Language—
   Mary Lou Cornejo
   Memories of a non-English speaker

Walking in Two Worlds—Angela Maria Jones
   Effect of community perceptions on being
   bilingual

El Norte (The North)

Mario A. Magaña

Childhood history

I was born in 1963 in the state of Michoacán, Mexico, in the very small community of Los Horcones, without running water or electricity. My mother and father are Mexicans. I have seven brothers and seven sisters. When I was 7, I began helping my father, brothers, and sisters to cultivate the land and raise milk cows. I attended 3 years of elementary school in my hometown and 3 years in a different school. My hometown elementary school at that time only offered classes through third grade. My second school was about 5 miles away. Sometimes we rode horses, bicycles, or walked.

Mexico is a wonderful place to live. The people are friendly. The weather is very nice. The food is delicious, with a large variety of tropical fruits. It is very difficult to live there, however, due to the unequal distribution of resources. The Mexican government is one of the most corrupt in the world. Mexico earns millions of dollars by exporting natural resources such as petroleum, gold, silver, copper, etc. The problem is that the profit from these resources gets distributed just among government administrators and a few wealthy businessmen.

I lived happily in Mexico until I was 18, when I began to notice that money was very important for survival. I started noticing big financial problems in my family. It did not matter how hard we worked, the money just was not enough to eat proper food or buy shoes and clothes. I remember that my father had only two changes of clothes because he was always broke.

When I was 20, I realized I had countless challenges ahead of me. Things were getting worse every month. Everything was too expensive. The unemployment rate was so high that it was almost impossible to find a job. The agricultural products that we harvested had no value on the market.

One day I was pasturing cows when my cousin Pedro Alvarez came to me and asked, "¿No te has cansado de olerles las nalgas a las vacas?" (Don't you ever get tired of smelling cows' bottoms?) I was not sure why he asked me this, but his point was that in the U.S. I could have a better life. He invited me to come with him, his brother, and another cousin to the U.S. He talked to me about new cars, clean places, nice clothes, easy-to-earn money, lots of beautiful, blonde girls, etc. He convinced me to come to this country.

The American (U.S.) dream
(El sueño norteamericano)

On a cold January morning, when the roosters started to crow, my mother very gently caressed my hair, shook my head, and woke me up. When I woke up, I noticed she was crying in silence. I asked her "¿Por qué lloras, mamá?" (Why are you crying, Mother?) She said, "Porque te vas, mi hijo, y no sé si te vuelva a ver." (Because you are leaving, my son, and I am not sure if I am going to see you again.) We hugged each other, and I said, "No te preocupes, mamá, te prometo que volveré muy pronto." (Do not worry, mother, I promise that I will return very soon.) I got up to get ready. I changed my clothes and ate a good breakfast because I might not eat again soon.

When I was ready to leave, my sisters began hanging from my neck, crying and begging me to stay in Mexico. My father said, "Cuídate mucho y nunca te olvides de tu mamá, escríbele cartas porque ella se preocupará mucho si no sabe nada de ti." (Take care of yourself and never forget your mother, write letters to her because she will worry if she does not hear anything from you.)

I was devastated for a few minutes, wondering if the North was worth my family's tears or my separation from my parents and siblings. On the other hand, my cousins were waiting for me. If I did not show up they would think I was a coward. I had given them my word, which is very important in the Mexican culture. Therefore, I decided to leave home.

I knelt in front of my mother and father and asked for their blessing. A soon as they finished, I made the sign of the cross and stood up. With my heart broken in a million pieces and my head down, I started walking toward the front door of our house. I turned around, waved my right hand, and walked toward my cousin's house three blocks down the street. I carried a plastic bag with one change of clothes. When I got to their house, I jumped in the back of my uncle's truck, and he drove us to the nearest town. At sunrise, we got to Tepalcatepec, where we got a bus to Tijuana.

Crossing the U.S. border

I arrived in Tijuana in the cold early morning of January 31, 1983. I had a thin jacket and one change of clothes. My cousins and I started walking the streets of Tijuana looking for a coyote (a person who helps undocumented people cross the U.S. border). In less than 2 hours, we found a coyote that charged $200 each. (I'm glad I crossed the border back then, because now they charge between $2,000 and $3,000 per person.)

The coyote took us to the isolated hills of Tijuana into a very dirty old garage, without running water, electricity, or bathrooms. There were more coyotes and about 40 other pollos (people trying to cross).

We stayed there for a few hours and about 6 p.m. started walking to be near the U.S.–Mexican border by nightfall. The darkness limits the vision of the U.S. Border Patrol officials. There, we waited until it got very dark; then we walked toward the U.S.–Mexican border. The coyote's goal was to get to Chula Vista, California, before dawn.

We walked and walked all night long. Along the way, we encountered many obstacles:

- *The cold.* I suffered cold as never before.

- *The rain.* It rained all night long. Just imagine yourself wet from head to toes, walking in regular shoes on a very steep, wet, grassy hill at night without a flashlight.

- *The dark.* I used to walk in the dark a lot, but when you are in danger on unknown ground, it is not easy. At times we were asked to run as fast as we could to cross large, open, grass fields, or to crawl for a mile or two through grass to stay hidden from the Border Patrol.

- *Border officials on horses.* We were chased by border officials on horses, but because we were many pollos (persons), I was able to escape every time. After they stopped chasing us, it was very difficult for us to get together again. A few people were captured, and others got lost. When we started, there were about 50 of us, and by the time we arrived at Chula Vista, there were about 20.

- *Border officials in helicopters.* There were a couple of helicopters patrolling the area with a powerful light attached beneath the helicopter. When we saw it coming, we immediately crawled under a bush, face down and did not move until the helicopter had gone.

- *Border officials in cars.* If the officials in the helicopters were able to see us, they dispatched officials in cars to capture us. The good thing was that there were between five and eight officials, not enough to capture all of us at the same time.

- *The distance.* Some of us were in good shape, but a few were not. I had to help my oldest cousin.

- *The residents of Chula Vista.* For me, this is the most incredible part of my story.

After walking, jogging, running, and crawling all night, we arrived at Chula Vista about 6 a.m. We were walking to a place where other coyotes had several cars waiting to take us to Los Angeles. The coyotes divided us into groups of four or five to minimize the impression that we were undocumented people on the streets. At that moment, the American dream seemed possible.

When we passed by some people playing basketball, one of them saw us and shouted, "¡Unos mojados! Llama a la migra." (Some wetbacks! Call the Border Patrol Office). The coyotes told us to go to somebody's house and hide under their bushes or knock on their door and ask permission to hide from the Border Patrol.

My cousins and I decided to run for a couple of blocks and hide behind a house with lots of bushes. In less than 5 minutes, several Border Patrol and police cars arrived and covered the area. In less than 10 minutes, all of us were captured and put in minibuses and taken to jail.

They kept us in jail for about 8 hours and then put us in a large bus and sent us back to Tijuana about 4 p.m. That night, we repeated the crossing. This time I had better luck.

The next day, my three cousins, four others, and I got a ride in the trunk of a car from Chula Vista to Los Angeles. They put us sideways so all of us could fit in the trunk. This was the most painful ride I ever had in my entire life because I was unable to move. I had one person in front of me, one in back, and another on top. The worst thing was that I was near the car's muffler. The heat from the muffler was burning my hip. I was unable to move. I tolerated the pain for 4 hours, the time it took us to get to Los Angeles. To me, it was like 4 million years.

Author's note: Mario began his life in the United States in 1983. With hard work and determination, he learned to read, write, and speak English and is now a citizen of the United States. He owns a home in Oregon where he, his wife, and three daughters reside. Mario completed his high school and college degrees in Oregon. He holds a master's degree from Oregon State University and is a successful OSU Extension 4-H faculty member.

Citizens League, a young civil rights organization with English-speaking leaders who staunchly supported America, urged the older Issei (first-generation immigrants) and their fellow JAs to comply with the evacuation orders as a way to demonstrate their faith in American democracy.

I had never experienced discrimination in Hawaii or on the mainland. But in 1972, I did. I was teaching at Parkrose Senior High School in Portland, Oregon. The faculty holiday gathering was scheduled at a fraternal lodge. When we approached, I noticed others signing in on a clipboard, waiting for a buzz, and then going through the double doors.

I signed in for my husband and myself and waited. No buzz. Instead, the woman asked who we were, why we were there, and the name of the member who had arranged the gathering. I gave answers to the first two questions, but didn't know the answer to the third. She asked more questions, and as the minutes passed, and we heard the buzz and watched the door open for others, we concluded that Japanese-Americans were probably not members or guests here.

We decided to leave just as another faculty member came through the entry doors. We explained why we were leaving, and he pshawed our decision, signed the clipboard, waited for the buzz, and to the chagrin of the receptionist, swept us through the door to join our party. I can still see the heads turn, much like those watching a tennis match, and feel the grip of my husband's hand in mine, telling me without words that it would be a short evening.

Almost 30 years later, I think of the vow I made that evening to treat every person with respect. Recently, in a suburban high school's faculty lounge, a professionally dressed woman sat working on a report. A visitor from an Educational Service District walked in. Without hesitation, the visitor said, "You must be the new English as a Second Language aide." She was quite taken aback when the woman answered that she was the school's vice-principal. Did I need to mention that the vice-principal was Asian? Stereotyping lives.

Going Shopping

Pamala Morris

This story begins with my assignment to the state 4-H/Youth department in Indiana. Being a member of the state staff meant that I was responsible for serving all 92 counties within the state. In order to serve as a resource person to county staff, I sometimes traveled to a specific county.

At the onset of my assignment, I used my personal car for these trips. However, I was quickly informed by my department head and several other administrators that it would be best for my safety to either take a university vehicle or ask people from the county to meet me in a centrally located place. I was informed it was not safe for African-Americans to venture into certain communities unless they were on official business. I was also told that I needed to inform certain county offices ahead of time about my visit so that the local police department would be on notice. Of course, this was really no surprise to me since I already was cognizant of the existing racial bias in the state.

With this bit of background information, I have decided to share my most recent experience. I was invited to attend a meeting that took place in a community just north of our capital city. Of course, I was professionally dressed that day since I was there on business.

After the meeting, I got into my car and proceeded to drive through the small town, when a store selling stained glass lamps caught my eye. I hesitated, as I usually do, and asked myself if it would be all right to get out of my car and browse around in the store. Would I be accepted as a customer, or would my presence be questioned? This was the kind of self-talk I seemed to have too often as I traveled to unfamiliar communities where people stared and frowned because I looked different from them.

Well, I decided to browse around in this very intriguing store to see if I could boost the economy. I walked in the store, and it seemed to be abandoned because I didn't see anyone and no one said anything to me. I proceeded to walk around until I heard the phone ring and someone picked it up. I looked over to the side, and there sat an elderly, gray-haired woman who then was forced to say hello. A few minutes later, a gentleman came rushing into the store as if he were looking for someone. When he spotted me, he smiled and walked immediately to the back of the store and held a conversation with the woman. Still, no one asked if they could help me as I continued to walk around.

I decided to leave the store, and the young man followed me out. He walked over to his truck and stood there until I was in my car. When I began to pull away from the curb, he pulled out in front of me and watched me continuously in his rear-view and side-view mirrors. I looked in my rear-view mirror and noticed that a policeman had driven up behind me. This may have been a coincidence, but I really doubt it. They sandwiched me between them until I made a turn to leave town. I was furious! This incident occurred in April 2001.

WHERE ARE YOU FROM?

By Sarah Harrison

Just last week I was walking into the grocery store after a long day at work. I was hoping to get in and out. My first stop was to pick up some bananas. I was looking forward to baking banana bread later that night. I could almost smell the warm bread in the air. I reached down to grab a plastic bag for the bananas and saw two beautiful blue eyes peering up at me.

My love for children drove my curiosity to say hello. For a few long seconds, the young girl stared at me in confusion yet interest because I look different than most people she sees. Her mouth opened and whispered, "Where are you from?" I was astounded by her words. How could such a small person know how to use such powerful words? Did she even know how hurtful and inappropriate her question was? I felt as if her words were sending me back to my alien planet, as if I didn't belong in the same store as her. This is something I deal with no matter where I go.

I remember while in college I once was having coffee with a good friend. Engaged in conversation, I barely felt the tap on my shoulder. I turned around, expecting to be greeted by another friend or coworker. Instead, an unfamiliar voice said, "I was very curious to know... where are you from?" I was confused as to why he didn't say hello first. Isn't that the more normal greeting?

Looking in the mirror, I see no difference from my peers, although my close friends would disagree with me. I am a registered Chippewa with the Turtle Mountain Indian Reservation in North Dakota.

My encounter with the young girl was just one of many since I was a young child. It is a question I just can't seem to get used to being asked. Each week, I have at least one person ask me the same question the young girl asked in the supermarket, "Where are **you** from?" It can be a young child to a grown adult. I could be at school, at the mall, or at a restaurant.

The first time I was asked, I didn't know how to react. Should I be mad or happy that people take an interest in my heritage? I soon learned that behind the question lies curiosity. So, for years I have been stuck with the dilemma of addressing when it is appropriate and when it is not to ask about someone's heritage.

It seems to me that "appropriateness" depends on several factors. The line between appropriate and inappropriate is very fine. The young girl in the supermarket was acting innocently, but in fact she was unskilled in watching her words. The man in the coffee shop probably had no grounds to ask. A coworker with whom I've established a relationship might simply be trying to get to know me better.

I have learned that curiosity-driven questions have to be asked with caution. My experiences have taught me to treat such difficult situations in the following ways. First, I establish a relationship with the person before asking questions of a personal nature. I always respect the person's right to privacy. I never push for more details than one desires to reveal. Lastly, I know that asking a stranger where he/she is from might be considered rude by the stranger.

Over the years, I have learned that life is purely a package of lessons, some for me to learn and others for me to teach. Up until now, I have been learning life's lessons. The most important lesson I have learned is that what I might see as normal is different than what someone else might see as normal.

Writing this story is my attempt to teach someone, just one person, a lesson that they will pass on to someone else. The lesson is that, when it comes to asking questions, every situation is different and depends on the existing relationship. When people ask, *"Where are you from?"* they might think they are being curious, but the question sometimes comes across as rudeness.

My first attempt at this story offended many people. They didn't understand why I could be so hurt by a young child's words. They would say, "It was a young child. How could you be upset when she didn't know any better?" The truth is that parents are not teaching their children appropriate words. If children don't learn to communicate effectively, they will grow up to be the adult in the coffee shop.

After much thought, I realized it wasn't the young girl in the story that disturbed people. It really came down to difference. They had never experienced the hurt I feel each day when someone confronts me about my difference.

I thought about how to rewrite the story so it didn't raise eyebrows. But, the truth was, I didn't want to. I had experienced these things and still do day in and day out. By sharing them, I might help people open their eyes and realize that what they do or say does rub off on their children. I only hope that people will gain a sense of what I experience and feel each time I am confronted with my difference.

I Decided to Wear African Attire

Kenneth Grimes

There was excitement in the air. A day of training was culminating in our annual Christmas party. I was Assistant Training Officer for a self-declared, progressive consulting firm that provided litigation support and software development for the Environmental Protection Agency. Besides officially coordinating new employee training and staff development, I also, unofficially, coordinated the annual Christmas party talent show. I recruited from more than 300 members of our staff that hailed from the 8 EPA regions and our Virginia headquarters.

The novelty of employees with "true" ability never ceased to amaze, even those who exhibited newfound talents each year. And I never ran out of "subjects" to work with because I knew secretly that everyone has gifts to share; it's just a matter of helping them rediscover them and hone them enough to put on display.

This event and preparing for it each year brought a new dimension to a highly technical, highly corporate culture. Again and again, our staff discovered that beyond the everyday amazing task of manipulating artificial intelligence and analyzing legal data, lay a fresh, new type of artistry and inventiveness as old as time.

The computer programmers had discovered the wherewithal on staff to create a five-piece rock band. Anticipation of their antics was the talk of the conference. People were going to be surprised that it wouldn't be a parody; these guys and one girl could jam. An administrative assistant with choir-directing experience decided that a number of us could tackle a portion of Handel's Messiah. A vice president took on his dream of being a stand-up comedian; a team leader showed off her juggling skills. There were surprisingly accomplished soloists and a makeshift crew of actors in a skit to highlight the year.

Of the 300+ employees, I was 1 of 2 persons of color working there. The other was another African-American, a woman who served as our extremely adept office manager. We worked closely together in all our daily activities and especially when coordinating the annual gathering. Denver was the unofficial headquarters, with the largest service center and most employees.

Things were in place. Training sessions had been organized. Our office manager had made all of the travel arrangements. Performers for a 45-minute show and a 30-minute rock set had received all the attention that could be mustered. It was in the hands of the universe.

I had decided I would wear African attire. This was the early '90s. I was proud of my heritage. It shouldn't be a big deal. The office manager and I sometimes spoke of how we had to suppress our cultural heritage, but we were loyal contributors to the success of the company. We didn't dwell on our difference, but we also didn't deny or try to hide who we were.

Still, there were daily incidents, insensitivities to what it meant to be two African-Americans in a company that had never employed "minorities" before. In a company made up of a large number of people barely out of college or from the suburbs of America, they admitted having very little experience with people that didn't look like them. The company didn't realize it, but there was an unwritten policy of "don't ask and don't tell," similar to that regarding gays in the military. Be Black, but don't be impositional about it.

No one was ever intentionally rude. Mostly there were stereotypes. Conversations would reveal that there was an assumption that life for the office manager and me must be difficult, because we, as other Blacks, must be from "the ghetto."

One day, a young couple came into my office, closing the door behind them so no one would overhear a breach of unspoken policy. They were rebels who were also secretly dating. "We saw 'Boyz in the Hood,'" the male confided, as if to say, "Now we understand what you have been going through." We talked. There was reality and unreality. It was an experience to be shared. Insights all around.

Frequently, when travel arrangements were made, the travelers wanted to know how to avoid the "bad neighborhoods," a catch phrase for ethnic communities. Less frequently, usually when discussing why we didn't need diversity training, someone would declare, "We're all human, right? Color doesn't matter."

They didn't realize that beyond the color was heritage, history, language, culture, the same as behind most of their names—Smith, Thomas, Earhardt. They didn't realize that behind the color was a different worldview. That was the link, not a denial of color but an acknowledgment of it that could bring about a greater empathy for one another, a deeper connection and another meaningful but alternate way of seeing things.

I had decided to wear African attire. Everyone was expected to dress up for the party—suits, ties, dresses, jewelry, shined shoes. I chose a traditional outfit from Ghana, West Africa, with a knee-length tunic that covered a pair of drawstring pants. Both were a brown, beige, and white pattern with purple highlights like expressive art. This was dress for the occasion in the homeland and in many African-American communities. I told my wife I was wearing African. She thought nothing of it. We often did so in that other world we lived in. She didn't know that my attire would be a lesson, that it would push the envelope of acceptance. She didn't realize that we would be chipping away at an unspoken policy that prevented the growth of more than 300 people and began with everyone who dared to ask "why?"

I would wear a kufi, a flat-topped hat worn in one form or another all around the continent—as Africa is commonly referred to by many African-Americans. I also wore a necklace made with cowry shells, which once served as money in some African countries but also represented fertility, synonymous with prosperity.

And finally, the entire ensemble was set off with a strip of kente cloth. Kente is an Asante ceremonial cloth that is handwoven in a large variety of patterns that serve as a visual representation of history, philosophy, ethics, oral literature, moral values, social code of conduct, religious beliefs, political thought, and aesthetic principles. Weaving is an honored tradition of the Akan peoples who live in parts of Ghana and Cote' d'Ivoire, where many slaves were forced onto ships and shuttled across the Atlantic Ocean.

Once only permitted for royalty or for special occasions, kente has become common in both Africa and America. One can tell what a person stands for or wants to express by what he or she wears, just as significantly as those who wear Nike, Calvin Klein, or Tommy Hilfiger. My kente pattern of orange, blue, shades of purple, and auburn was called Adwinasa (a'djwin a' sah), symbolizing royalty, elegance, creative ingenuity, excellence, wealth, perfection, and superior craftsmanship.

"How do I look?" I asked my wife.

"Okay," she replied, which for her meant more than the word; if anything were out of place, she would let me know in no uncertain terms. I had even shined my shoes.

We entered the ballroom of the hotel where the party was held. The room was dazzling with black, white, blue, and gray suits and glittering red, green, yellow, and sequined gold and silver dresses. The talent show participants rushed us with last minute "crises."

As my wife and I moved toward the stage, the president of the company moved toward us. He was a striking, country gentleman with graying temples and a fatherly manner. He prided himself on knowing every employee by first name even though he was headquartered in Virginia and we were in eight regions. He had demonstrated this gift at one of our Christmas parties. It was supposed to be a demonstration of how much he cared about each one of us or to solidify his corporate image as a leader. Moving toward us, I thought I saw an angry glint in his eye.

"What's with the costume?" he asked in a tone that was only mildly diplomatic.

Ah, the lesson began, and at the top. "It's a traditional outfit from Ghana. The kente cloth is a special weave of the Akan people. The pattern is called adwinasa and stands for royalty, elegance...."

We strode toward the stage, him to welcome everyone, me to introduce talent wearing my "costume."

P.S. In the following 2 years, the company hired two more African-Americans, three individuals of Latin heritage, two Asians, and one Native American. I had the honor of training them all.

THE BEAUTY OF DIFFERENCE

Steve Hanamura

During my high school and college years, a primary concern for me was whether I could belong to a group or fit in with others. The need to fit in or belong is not unique to me, but perhaps what is different is the reason for my concern.

Blind from birth, I learned very early that I was different. I went to a residential school for the blind, which meant that I lived away from home since the age of 5 for 9 months out of the year. While sighted children were playing sports and doing lots of things at home, my being away at school highlighted that I was clearly different from most other kids my age.

I remember my parents telling me that I would need to grow up and become successful. "You need to get a college education and you will have to work twice as hard as sighted people." The teachers and counselors at the school for the blind reinforced this comment.

Upon graduating from the ninth grade, I continued my education at a public high school, which meant that I would be mixing in with sighted students. This was very scary. A major breakthrough came for me when I was able to join the choir. I was finally involved in a meaningful way with students who could see. Our collective differences, though evident, were overridden and acknowledged by a director who knew how to help the sighted students be with me and me with them. It was a marvelous experience during my 3 years in school. I still did not have a good feeling about who I was, but at least I was becoming involved in society.

During my senior year, I heard about Linfield College in McMinnville, Oregon. They had a great choir and were known for taking tours. "Wow," I thought to myself, "that sounds like fun." I knew that I would have to audition, but it was worth a try.

Off to Linfield I went, with hopes of joining the Acapella Choir. It worked for me in high school, so it should work for me again in college. I went through auditions for choir and was disappointed to learn that I didn't get in.

My disappointment for not getting in turned to feelings of being shattered when I found why I wasn't selected. There were two openings for bass singers, and three of us who tried out. One singer was outstanding and clearly deserved to get in. The second singer and I were fairly equal, and it could have gone either way.

The director was afraid that I wouldn't be able to find the bathrooms on choir tour. He was nervous that I would be a burden to my classmates, who would have to help me, and that I would be an embarrassment in the host homes where we would stay. I had come all the way from California to join the choir, and then this. I was devastated.

I spent that year singing in the College Choir, a step down from Acapella and no tours. I made sure I sat right in front of the director so he could see how I learn music. I had words written down in Braille and made sure it was visible to him. I sang with our fraternity and became a member of a folk singing group on campus. We became fairly well known.

When auditions came around the next year, over half of the Acapella Choir went to the director on my behalf. They told him that they would see to it that I could find the bathrooms and that whoever roomed with me at a host home would also make sure that I wouldn't be too much trouble to our host families. The director by this time had seen me function. I got into Acapella, and we have become good friends with a high degree of respect for each other.

Upon leaving Linfield, I still had some work to do around how I felt about being different. I actually turned my back on singing for a few years because I didn't want to be stereotyped with Stevie Wonder, José Feliciano, or Ray Charles. That was my problem, not anyone else's.

I eventually got through those feelings and returned to singing because it is part of who I am and something I like to do. I needed to be willing to be out there so others could experience my capabilities and then allow the selection process for other choirs to take its own course.

Not all people who are different are superstars. I am a fairly good singer who can provide a solid contribution to a choir, but I am not an outstanding singer. The beauty of difference is when all differences can come together to make harmony. That's what belonging to a choir is about—sopranos, altos, tenors, and basses all coming together to make beautiful music.

THE EFFECT OF SPANISH AS MY FIRST LANGUAGE

Mary Lou Cornejo

There are so many memories to draw from, and yet those that remain the strongest in my mind are those that impacted me the most. These events can follow you for the rest of your life. One of these events was when my father took me to school for the first time. All my young life, my grandmother and dad had coddled me, shown me love, held me up— and then I went to school.

My first day of school, I can remember the fear that I felt being in an alien environment that I did not know. I always took it for granted that everyone spoke Spanish. Little did I know that this was not the case and that I would suffer immensely at the hands of the teacher that I was told was to be respected. The Mexican culture holds educators in high esteem. They are viewed as demigods who can do no wrong and who are there to instill education and values in children. What is also instilled is that the teacher is never wrong; after all, she is the guardian of the gates to education!

Alas, the things we inadvertently do to our children. On my first day, I met my teacher, Mrs. King. She was skinny, old, had brown hair, wore glasses, and had such a distasteful look upon her face. What a shock; no one spoke Spanish! I can still see myself sitting at a table and not understanding a word that she was saying. Or for that matter, not understanding anyone. Even though there were other Mexican children, no one spoke to me in Spanish. Little did I know that they didn't dare, because they would be hit.

This was the case with Mrs. King. Because she could not communicate with me, she would slap my face and pull my hair. This was done in front of the other children. Of course, some of them, seeing how she treated me, would also hit, punch, or kick me with no consequences from Mrs. King. I remember that first time and the many others and how helpless I felt knowing I could not defend myself. I remember sobbing with the feelings of shock and shame when this happened to me. When I told my father, he said, "Tell your teacher I don't send you to school to be hit." I don't know what planet he was on at the time, but I could not articulate this to the teacher since I did not know English.

I specifically remember one time coming back from the gym. I was daydreaming and ran into some barbed wire that was lying on the ground. I ended up with deep scratches and the blood flowing from them, and my teacher saying, "That will teach you to pay attention to where you are going." What she did not realize was that most of the time I was day-dreaming to escape from her and the other children's abuse!

I also remember the look on the other teachers' faces. I would pass them in the hall on my way to the classroom or out to play, and their looks told me how sorry they were for me, but still no one intervened.

This event was to haunt me the rest of my school life and into adulthood. The feeling of not being good enough still persists in everything I do, even though I have won numerous awards in military and civilian life! I find that I strive to do better and am never satisfied. I have continued the cycle with my children, who for a long while felt nothing they did ever satisfied me.

Walking in Two Worlds

Angela Maria Jones

I have read the numerous *Letters to the Editor* printed in the local newspaper over the past few months. The topic has been people in our community speaking Spanish in public.

I recall it began with an acrid letter written by a woman who was upset that two women and some children were having a conversation in Spanish. The conversation, which occurred in a public place, took place in close proximity to the woman. She was angry that these people were in the United States and had the audacity to be speaking in Spanish. According to her quasi-standards, those individuals should stop speaking Spanish and learn to speak English because they are in the United States.

Since that letter, many citizens of our town have responded with their own points of view on this topic—some in agreement and some in disagreement. I have lived in this community long enough to know that the number of folks in agreement might not be many, but they are vocal. I have experienced my share of discrimination in this community, and it saddens me to read the letters in support of the woman's complaint. The situation brings two stories to mind.

I was at the movie theater with my father. We were chatting, as most people do, before the movie started. We began to reminisce about my grandparents. I barely remember my grandmother, but when my father started talking about her I could feel the warmth and love emanating from his face. He began to describe her beauty. He talked about my grandmother's many admirers and how my grandfather courted her. He had a far-off look as if he were seeing my grandmother in his mind's eye. I noticed that while he was painting her portrait for me, he had switched from English to Spanish. You see, my father and I are bicultural and bilingual. We were born in the United States and grew up speaking both English and Spanish. His parents taught him, and my parents taught me.

As I have read the various letters in the newspaper, the picture of my father and myself sitting in the movie theater comes to mind. I am filled with sadness and frustration, because no one has the right to tell my father he must recount for me the images of his mother, his childhood, my childhood, my heritage, my culture in English.

I spoke with a group of women last night in an effort to coordinate some English conversation classes through the town's university. There were seven women present. Four were working mothers who did not speak English. Three were third-year Spanish students. The three students were there to offer to work with these mothers to learn English. Not just to learn colors or the days of the week, but the English that is important to those mothers. Those parents want to have conversations with their children's teachers. They want to be able to communicate with the grocery store clerk. They want to be able to ask for an employment application.

As the discussion progressed, the moms talked about their discrimination experiences. They talked about the harassment received for not knowing the English language. Yet, not one was angry at having been treated poorly. Instead, they focused on their desire to learn English, such a strong desire that it is not uncommon for people to attend ESL classes at various locations.

These stories bring up some very real concerns. I know that as human beings we automatically respond to certain circumstances based on our past experiences. Sometimes that's important, as in learning not to touch a hot stove. And sometimes it's not the wisest choice, as in *assuming* that a person who is brown-skinned with dark hair and is speaking Spanish *does not* speak English.

You *might* be able to guess by looking at me that I speak Spanish, but should you assume that I do not speak English? I live, work, play, read, write, worship, eat, and breathe in English *and* in Spanish. I enjoy both of my cultures. Each helps to define the person I am. I cannot help but think how much richer in spirit I am to have in me the gifts of my American and Mexican cultures.

But still I am bothered. It bothers me that there are community members who do not care if I have anything to contribute because I might not be able to express myself in English. And it should bother all of us that so many members of my community (and others) are willing to let this unfair treatment continue.

I wish we could somehow challenge everyone to take off their blinders and look at the entire horizon, so that they can see the sun of opportunity rising. The opportunity to learn from each other. The opportunity to demonstrate courtesy and respect. Perhaps, even the opportunity to teach someone the English language.

We are living history, folks. Our horizon is changing. It is bright and full of colors. May those who see the sun continue their efforts to help others live, work, and play in whatever language they choose.

GROWING UP ADOPTED

Marion Isherwood

My family fulfills the requirement of what it means to be a melting pot. To begin with, none of us were born in the United States. My parents were both born in England, my brother was born in Nepal, and I was born in Bangladesh. Sam, my brother, and I were both adopted from our native countries when we were only a few weeks old. Neither of us has spent much time in either Nepal or Bangladesh. The essence of our native cultures still intrigues both of us, but we were not raised learning a lot about the way our lives could have been.

Throughout most of my life so far, I've managed to be able to feel like I blend in with the people around me even though I am different. I do realize that on the outside I look different, but I was raised just like any other American girl. I always have had everything I needed and much more. I've been blessed to have parents who love me, even though they are not my biological parents.

Even though I consider myself just like everybody else, though, there are reminders here and there that make it impossible to forget that I am different. After all, the town I was raised in only had about one or two people in each grade that were not some form of European mix.

One of the most vivid memories I have of trying to understand why I am different was when I was in seventh grade. I had a friend that I considered to be one of my closest friends when I started middle school. One day my father and I decided to invite my friend to go on a hike with us. She was able to go until we went to pick her up. Her mother looked at me with a strange expression on her face. I did not fully understand why she was so shocked. She forbade my friend to come hiking with me because she told me there were too many bears in the woods. I never really considered the bears to be a problem.

The next day in school, my friend told me her mom was uncomfortable with me because I was "black" and that she needed to get used to me. I was old enough to comprehend what this meant, but I had never really had to face my being different in a situation like this.

In the past, I had people point and say, "Do you see her, she's black." I even remember telling people when I was little that I was not black, but that I was brown. However, saying that I am brown would not help this situation. The effects of this experience still tug on me today. I struggled with keeping our friendship close. I really wanted to understand what her mother was thinking, but it created a wall between my friend and me.

Last summer, I went through a different experience of trying to fit in. I went to Bangladesh for the first time since I was a baby. I found myself in a place where I looked just like everyone else on the streets. People expected me to know the culture. They expected me to know the language. I did not know much about either of these things. It was a different kind of challenge. I loved being able to see what other Bengali girls my age looked like. I also enjoyed being able to be thankful for the life that I do have. We visited villages that were in a similar kind of poverty as the one my birth mother was from.

My differences in Bangladesh were flip-flopped from my differences in the United States. There I looked like everyone else, but I have a Western woman's attitude. I shocked some of the people in Bangladesh with the way I am. There were positive shocks and negative ones. Muslim men looked down upon me because I was wandering around with older American men. Young women were impressed with my freedom and joy for life. It was an encouragement to them to see a Bengali woman coming back to visit their country.

Even though I might never fit in completely in either setting, the United States or Bangladesh, I still am happy with the way my life is. I could not have imagined a better family. We all fit together nicely, and our differences create a colorful picture. I always will be able to compare my looks to the Bengalis and my culture to the Americans. I am blessed to be a little bit of two very different worlds.

"Homo"genized

Michael G. Keller, M.A.

I was born in 1952 and raised in Ohio for 18 years. I think I was around 7 years old when I first heard the word "homo," but I did not know what it meant. From the reaction of my father, I suspected it was not a good thing—his face became all red, his forehead wrinkled into a frown, his fists were clenched, and his eyes became tight and fixed, steely like his loud and grinding voice.

In fifth grade, I was still in the "C" room—that was the way we were categorized in those days, clumped together by our performance. Maybe that was easier for the teachers to teach to, or maybe it was easier to keep us in our place. Whatever the reason, that was the year I had my first male teacher, Mr. B., and he was the greatest! He was my homeroom teacher and my math teacher. He paid attention to me, giving me projects to do, help when I needed it, and he ran a tight ship when it came to discipline. I think that because he was kindhearted, I wanted to both learn *and* perform well for him. As a result, he recommended that I be moved into the "A" room in sixth grade. I stayed an "A" student from that time onward.

In seventh grade, the hormones were starting to rage, and all around me was the "coupling" adventure. Girls had always been easy for me to be around and to talk to, so playing the coupling game was simple for me. Actually, I was able to fit in like everyone else. Except that I wanted to spend all of my time with my best friend, Joey. We did everything together. I look back on him as my first real "crush." And I wanted more than just to be friends, but he didn't.

By age 15, I knew that I could get dates with girls and "pretend" to be sexually interested like all the other guys. I could "pass" as a normal guy. But I knew that I was different in ways that were not easy to ignore or change. I fantasized romances with cute guys with tight, muscled bodies, auburn hair, and blue eyes. I wanted men that would care for me; share their passion and adventure, their vulnerability; be daring and rebellious, yet gentle and trustworthy. I wanted their attention, their affection, their acceptance of me. But they were preoccupied with getting chicks and getting laid.

By age 16, I stopped going to church. It was clear from repeated sermons and innuendoes that loving another man—as a woman—was a clear route to ridicule, rejection, hell-fire, and eternal damnation, an overwhelming and unacceptable fate for me...and I didn't even believe it was true. So, I kept my yearnings to myself. I found (and still find) it an irreconcilable duality that God somehow would always "love me" but damn my "love" for men.

I managed to survive high school, faked a few "serious" relationships with women, and had my first sex in a committed relationship with another man. That's when I finally "knew" I was gay. There was no going back, *and* I had no idea how to go forward.

Unfortunately, I still chose to hide and pretend that I was "normal" (read "heterosexual"), secretly hoping for my white knight to come and carry me away to a place where we could live and love without fear. I held onto that quiet dream of being rescued (from myself and from my pain) until I chose to "come out" when I was 30.

For the most part, my coming out to the world (and to terms with) my sexuality was a freeing and rejuvenating experience. I found that many folks were "surprised" and had no idea; some were angry that I had "lied" to them all these years. Others were relieved to have the truth. The spell of years living with my "internalized homophobia" had been broken.

With my newfound freedom (and a boyfriend in tow), I decided to travel overseas for a year, exploring new landscapes and exotic cultures—clearly a metaphor for negotiating my new lifestyle—an opportunity to be who I am with mostly anonymity.

Ironically, I ended up living in rural Asia for 10 years, where I was accepted by the locals and by my compatriots. In essence, I recreated myself, evolved bicultural values, learned new customs and social practices. I journeyed inward to open my heart to loving myself unconditionally and, thereby, to accepting every human being as a precious gift—discovering a vast potential for "being" human.

While I was living overseas, the "gay epidemic" of AIDS was rapidly spreading, infecting individuals and society in irreversible ways. Once again, the religious right was damning gay men for their affliction and abandoning them through their righteousness. I was frightened and confused, shocked, and saddened. During my visits back to the States each summer, more of my friends were becoming sick and dying. Somehow, I was spared the disease, but not the guilt of being a survivor.

My overseas experience was liberating for my soul and revitalizing for my integrity as a conscious human being! I had challenged my home culture norms, my limited ways of thinking and viewing myself and others— gotten outside of my box—and I crafted a blend that worked for me.

Upon returning to live in America, I found myself once again in a very different context. As an "older" and single gay man, it seemed that I was relegated to a life of solitude, des- tined only to volunteer for organizations dedi- cated to representing and supporting gays and lesbians as valued human beings in society. And I still had questions: How was I going to meet other gay men? How was I going to inte- grate my overseas experience into my lifestyle back home? Had I become too "eccentric" from my experiences to be accepted and appreciated by other gay men?

In my workplace, as an academic, there seemed more general acceptance of my being gay, even though I was the only openly gay male faculty member on campus. I noticed that some of my former internalized homophobia was resurfacing: Could I be fired? Would students complain about me or make false accusations? Would other faculty and staff shun me?

Fortunately, there were a number of lesbian faculty who were very open and apparent on campus. In short, their support helped me shake off that old pattern of self-deprecation and stand solidly in the realization that I am more than what others think of me; I am more powerful than my fear; and I am a lovable, capable, whole, and magnificent human being!

Clearly, while I was growing up, there were no gay support groups, no GLBT (Gay, Lesbian, Bisexual and Transgender) community centers, no Gay-Straight Alliance in the schools, no "gay-friendly" TV programs, no PFLAG (Parents, Families and Friends of Lesbians and Gays) for parents of gays, and no public celebrations honoring gay authors, artists, or community leaders. The contexts continue to change, and what is important is how we choose to respond. And so it goes for all of us: each context calls forth another "lens" through which I and we view each other, assess our values, interpret our behavior, and make our choice about how much love we want to bring into our world together.

Being gay is only one aspect of the unique "me" or "we" or "us" in any one setting. However, being gay is an important and elemental aspect of who I am and how I self-identify in the world. Like each of us, my self-image often determines my degree of self-expression and my creative contribution.

My being gay is not a "threat" to humanity; it is threatening only to those who are unwilling to recognize my humanity. I want and deserve love and acceptance to no greater or lesser degree than anyone else.

There always have been and always will be gay children growing up in predominantly non-gay households. As a result, I am committed through my work to creating space for all to find and express their unique voice and unconditional love! For it is through our differences that we are most alike; through our love that we unite our hearts and dream our loftiest dreams of all that we can be!

LOOKS CAN BE DECEIVING

Vivian Aguilera

I have spent much of my life finding my place in the different worlds to which I belong. People's usual perception of me—especially if I am without a partner or other person who might give me away—is that I am white, American-born, straight, middle class, female, and young.

The truth is that I identify as Latina, Spanish, bisexual, middle class, female, and older than I look. But much to the comfort of the mainstream, I pass as mainstream and have therefore been privy to and horrified by the comments people make when they are with one of their own.

Where'd you learn to speak Spanish so well?

"Passing" is something I struggle with in nearly every community with which I come into contact. I am fortunate to have a Spanish-by-way-of-Cuba last name that affords me the privilege of being considered Latina by other Latinos. After living in the States for most of my life, my Spanish accent is a mish-mosh of my Spanish and Cuban heritage sprinkled with some Mexican words and phrases I've learned along the way in my professional life as a therapist.

Although Spanish is my first language, I have been asked countless times where I learned to speak Spanish so well. This question is insulting to me because I have great pride in being a Spanish citizen (despite living in the U.S. for nearly 25 years) and in being able to maintain my first language when so many other young immigrants lose that ability as they grow older.

Because of my white skin and features, I find myself trying to explain my right to call myself Latina within the Spanish-speaking community. But I also find myself trying to show my uniqueness in the white world. I do not want to be considered one of "them" even by them.

At my last workplace, I was respected by those in power (all white, mostly male) because I am "educated" and I speak English well, and if they looked superficially enough they saw no trace of an immigrant or a person different than them. I got the television references, I know most of the songs they remember, and I got their jokes (though I sometimes was offended by them). But when things came up where I advocated for one of my own, I lost standing and risked being labeled a troublemaker like the Latinos who had spoken up before me.

"Dime con quien andas, y te diré quien eres."

The other two worlds I navigate are the queer and straight worlds. In general, bisexuality is little understood either by those who identify themselves as exclusively straight or those who identify themselves as exclusively gay/lesbian. There are all sorts of misconceptions of what it means.

Just as with many other groups, bisexuality means different things for each bisexual. For me, I identify as "bi" because it makes the most sense to me in honoring the relationships I've had in my life. I have had straight partners and lesbian partners and I cared for them all. I do not have a stronger preference for one gender or one sexual orientation. Yet, this is of great interest and perplexity to others.

There is a saying in Spanish, *"Dime con quien andas, y te diré quien eres,"* which roughly translates to, "Tell me who you are with, and I'll tell you who you are." My mom used this during my teen years to discourage me from hanging out with friends she perceived to be delinquents or drug addicts. However, in my coming-out years it has taken on a new meaning.

When I told my mother that I was bi, she urged me to find a man to marry because, after all, if I really didn't care about gender, what was the harm in finding a soul mate who was a man? I told her I didn't think it worked that way. My choosing of a partner, she needed to understand, would be based on my relationship with that person regardless of their gender. Her response was, "Well, if it's a woman, everyone will think you are a lesbian." And, she's right.

I had a lesbian partner who said, "I don't understand why you have to tell people you are bisexual if you are with me. Doesn't that make you a lesbian?" I explained that by that reasoning I would only be defined by who or what my partner is, and that wasn't acceptable to me. She said, "Well, I think you are splitting hairs there."

Today, I am married to a wonderful woman with whom I plan to spend the rest of my life. We plan to raise children together. And to everyone outside of those who know, we are a lesbian couple. To our neighbors, we are the lesbian couple who live in the complex. To some of my coworkers, I am "the lesbian in the office." At gay and lesbian pride parades and dyke marches, I am a lesbian. In the mainstream, to men who don't know better (when I am not holding my partner's hand), I am another straight girl who deserves to be called "baby" and "sweet thing."

Straight women in meetings or in a waiting room ask me what my husband does. When telemarketers ask for my partner and I tell them "she isn't available," they ask me if her husband is. Sometimes I say, "You're speaking to her." Often, they hang up. When Becky and I are together in public and not visibly affectionate, people ask us if we are sisters. When I feel safe enough, I say, "No, we're gay." I find people don't have a good response to that. Usually the best they can muster is, "Oh, you are?"

The sad thing about this is that I often just identify myself as gay or lesbian to others because it's easier for them to understand. And if I identified within myself as lesbian, I would be proud of it. But I don't. My experience is different, and I am not being true to myself when I explain myself in ways that are more palatable to those who don't know better. But those are some of the battles one chooses not to fight.

To the guy at the gas station who asked if we were roommates, I said, "No, we're partners." He said, "Oh. OK" and walked away. He returned 10 seconds later and said, "What do you mean, partners?" And I had a choice there. I could say, "Well, you see, sir, my partner, Becky, who just went inside to pay for gas, is a lesbian. I myself am bisexual, which to me means I am equally attracted to men and women, but I have fallen in love with Becky, so I am in a relationship with her. We plan to have children together and live happily ever after." Or I could say, "We're lesbians." I chose the latter, and, frankly, that was already more than the gentleman could handle.

So, I have to find a sense of peace within myself. I have to decide when it's OK to misrepresent who I am for the greater good and for my own safety. And I guess as long as I know who I am and how I feel and those who love me and support me also know, that's the most important part. But I also have a long way to go in the educating of others of what bisexuality is and why it's not OK to lump us all into one group based on who our partners are. That's the work I have in front of me.

Out of Place in Selma

Michael Kirk

I grew up in small-town America, in predominantly white, middle-class neighborhoods. Living in the Pacific Northwest, I had never been to the deep South, but recently I had the chance to go and see a civil rights reenactment. I was with a group of people whom I had just met. They seemed friendly enough; they did not exclude me from group activities even though I was the only male under 20. I was excited to experience history personally.

The town of Selma was not unlike any other town in America. It had shops along the street with people milling about in an open-air market. My group walked down to the Brown Chapel A.M.E. to experience the rally that led up to the bridge-crossing in Selma. I am not extremely extroverted in large crowds, but I do feel a sense of confidence in the way I act in most situations. When we arrived at the chapel after a 10-minute walk, there was a crowd of almost a thousand people gathered around the steps, waiting for the activity to commence. I walked up onto the steps of the chapel, following the rest of our group, to keep some sense of connection with at least the surrounding people.

Before the group had a chance to head inside the church, singing started in the crowd on the steps about 10 feet from where I stood. The music slowly silenced everybody and at the same time gave them all one voice. Everyone started to sing. The song was a song of struggle and persistence in the style of a spiritual call and response. I did not know the song. I had no voice in the crowd.

As I looked over the people gathered, I began to notice something. I found I was one of about 100 white people in a crowd of a thousand. Then I noticed something further: I was the only white person in his teens. As the first song came to a close and the next song began, I started to feel very out of place. Now I not only had no voice, but I did not even look like I had a voice.

A new emotion seized me: fear—a fear that I did not belong here; a fear that the crowd would blame me for their struggles to overcome discrimination solely because I did not suffer with them. The other people who looked like me seemed to be doing all right. I remember thinking they seemed to be able to relate because they had lived during the civil rights movement so they could sympathize.

I felt alone in the crowd. I did not know what to say, or sing in this case, how to act, or what to think. My self-confidence was gone. I was stripped of everything that made me feel that I was a person who mattered. I did not have anything or anyone left but myself. I became very introverted. If someone had come up to talk to me, they would have thought that I was apathetic to the whole situation. It was not that I didn't care, but that I didn't know how to care.

Speeches came after the spirituals. People were cheering and ready to go fight for their rights once again, while my feelings of self-worth had been stripped away to almost nothing. One speech that made me know that I was not entirely alone in my feelings was by Congressman Dick Gephardt. He was the only white person to address the crowd. In contrast to his actions, he was very uncomfortable as well. That speech struck me because I had just seen him confidently addressing the nation on TV a few weeks before.

Finally, the crowd broke up and paraded down toward the bridge for the ceremonial crossing. As quickly as possible, I retreated. I found the one person who made me feel like a significant being again, my mother. By that time the experience was becoming a blur.

After I returned home, people asked me what my experience was. What was I supposed to tell them? Awful? I ended up just saying, "Fine," and telling them about the speeches that took place and the other easily explained ideas.

Now that I think back on the ordeal, I can see that I found out more about the civil rights movement than just the history of it. I found out what it was like to be an outsider in my own country. I found out how, just by the way we look and act, not even with malicious intent, we can make a person nothing. I discovered within myself what it is like to be a minority in a society. I cannot imagine what it must be like to experience that feeling every day of one's life. I also discovered that only in the arms of someone who truly cares can I overcome the feeling of being alone.

Section Five

Continuing the Learning

If I stay with the emerging conversation,
my own voice deepens and grows richer.
It is then that I begin to use
what I have learned,
to blend it, to mold it, to adapt it,
to integrate it.

Bernice McCarthy
About Learning

Chapter 12

HOW TO EXPERIENCE DIFFERENCE FROM HOME

The more you experience cultural difference, the more you can see and understand differences in communication styles.

People of different gender, physical abilities, sexual orientation, and age have always been among us. Now, with rapidly growing Latino, Asian, and other immigrant populations, it is becoming easier to meet people of different racial, ethnic, and national backgrounds. Thus, there are many opportunities to experience cultural difference right in our own communities.

Short of walking up to a stranger in a grocery store and striking up a conversation, here are five ways to experience difference from home and a sixth way for the traveler.

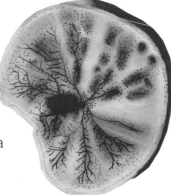

ASK SOMEONE YOU KNOW WHO IS FROM A DIFFERENT CULTURE

If you have a friend, acquaintance, or colleague who is culturally different from yourself, you have a wonderful opportunity to learn. People like to talk about themselves, but it is important to ask questions respectfully and in an appropriate time and place.

There are appropriate and inappropriate questions to ask. I try to stay away from questions that ask "why" because they can easily put someone on the defensive. "Why" questions shut down conversations rather than open up a dialogue.

Here are some appropriate questions to get started:

I noticed that you…(describe an observed behavior). Can you tell me what this means?

Tell me more about….

What does it mean in your culture when someone says (or does)...?

What is the experience of living in this community like for you?

What are some of the most difficult adjustments you have had to make while living in this town?

What do you see as the biggest differences between our two cultures?

What do you wish we understood about your culture?

What do you think is important for me to know about...?

Remember that culture is so deep that people often are not aware of their own. People can talk about their experiences, however. Being open to the stories of others is a very powerful and informative experience. To me, it is the key to cross-cultural understanding.

TALK WITH A CULTURAL INFORMANT— SOMEONE WHO KNOWS THE DIFFERENCES BETWEEN TWO CULTURES

A cultural informant is someone who is bicultural and either is from or has lived extensively in the culture you want to learn about. Cultural informants are bridge-builders. They can walk in two worlds with a conscious understanding of the differences. Thus, they can help both cultures understand each other.

If you meet someone who is comfortable and confident in your culture as well as in the one you want to learn about, you most likely have met a potential cultural informant. Ask your questions respectfully in the right time and place. Even ask what you think are dumb questions.

OBSERVE OTHERS

Once you have some culturally specific information
(or the information from
Section Two of this book),
watch how people from other cultures
behave. Describe in your mind what you see
before trying to interpret it. Remember the
example of the bell curve—not all people
from a given cultural group always behave
according to the cultural generalization for
that group.

WATCH MOVIES ABOUT OTHER CULTURES

Your closest video rental store is filled with cross-cultural adventures. One could argue that all films are cross-cultural. Many contain beautiful examples of the values and communication styles described in this book.

Some films perpetuate stereotypes in an attempt to be funny. If you question the validity of how a film portrays a certain cultural group, ask a cultural informant for clarification.

Most of the films listed here can be found in the drama or comedy sections of your local video store. The foreign film section might have others.

When you watch a film, become aware of variations in values and communication styles. Look for evidence of these variations in the characters and settings. Watch a film more than once and discuss the differing styles and patterns with someone.

Here are a few of my favorites.

Native American/Canadian

I Heard the Owl Call My Name (1973). Set in an isolated Indian village in British Columbia, a naïve young Anglican priest is caught between his worldview and that of the village people. Pay close attention to the scene in which the Anglican priest asks, "How big is your village?" I see this exchange as a struggle to translate high-context thinking into terms that a low-context thinker can understand.

Pow Wow Highway (1989). This little-known gem shows how contemporary Native Americans face dilemmas in their community. My favorite line is "My pony threw me!"

Mexican/Mexican-American/Guatemalan

The Ballad of Gregorio Cortez (1983). Based on a real-life story. Gregorio Cortez was arrested in 1901 as a suspected horse thief. Unable to speak English, Cortez fights off the authorities, who speak very poor Spanish. The most powerful line in the movie for me was "¿Por eso?"

Like Water for Chocolate (1993). The story of a young woman who learns to suppress her passions under the eye of a stern mother. The title is a common Spanish expression, "Como agua para chocolate," which means someone is very hot or angry. The movie opens with a symbolic metaphor. Watch for intense value statements.

Mi Familia (1995). Young José Sanchez tires of the turmoil and lack of work in Mexico and decides to head north to a "little village called Los Angeles." Having no sense of geography, he figures he can walk there in about a week. The story unfolds years later as his children struggle to adjust in a world of two cultures.

A Walk in the Clouds (1995). Paul Sutton, who has just returned home from the Army during World War II, takes a job as a salesman peddling chocolates. He encounters a Mexican-American woman and becomes involved with her family, who owns and operates a large vineyard. Watch for deep-seated values in this beautiful story.

The Milagro Beanfield War (1988). This story is about community activism in a small New Mexico town. Community members are caught between a local farmer who needs water for his bean field and a real estate developer who controls the water. Watch the power dynamics unfold.

El Norte (1983). A Guatemalan Indian brother and sister are forced, after the politically motivated murder of their father, to seek shelter outside their village, so they head to the U.S. with no visas. Look for wonderful examples of differences in Anglo and Guatemalan values and communication styles. The washing machine scenes are funny and instructive. This film is hard to find, but worth the search.

Chinese/Chinese-American/Japanese-American

The Joy Luck Club (1993). This story about four Chinese-American mothers and their daughters is set in San Francisco. It is filled with miscommunication that stems from differing worldviews. There are some funny scenes of cultural miscommunication, especially the dinner scene with the Anglo boyfriend.

Shower (1999). In a decaying neighborhood in Beijing, a local bathhouse serves as a meeting place for the elderly men of the community. The movie portrays beautiful examples of individualism and collectivism as well as high-context and indirect communication styles. Pay close attention to the sense of belonging that Erming, a mildly retarded son, has in the community.

Crouching Tiger, Hidden Dragon (2000). Set in the early 19th century, this Chinese film is filled with beautiful examples of values that reflect a sense of duty and a virtuous long-term orientation. There also are lots of examples of high-context and indirect communication throughout the film. Watch for the scene where the teacup is dropped.

Come See the Paradise (1990). After the bombing of Pearl Harbor, a Japanese-American wife and daughter are placed in an internment camp and are separated from their white, union-organizing husband/father.

African-American

Jungle Fever (1991). African-American director Spike Lee examines the repercussions of an interracial relationship upon two very distinct communities. Watch for the well-known scene in which the African-American women talk about the affair.

Do the Right Thing (1989). Spike Lee addresses racial and social ills, using as his springboard the hottest day of the year on one block in Brooklyn, NY. Three businesses dominate the block: a storefront radio station, where a smooth-talkin' African-American DJ spins the platters that matter; a convenience store owned by a Korean-American couple; and Sal's pizzeria, the only white (Italian)-operated business in the neighborhood.

Save the Last Dance (2001). An inner-city high school sets the stage for African-American communication dynamics in a cross-cultural setting. The last dance in the movie is a beautiful example of how effective cross-cultural communication results in the creation of something new and exciting.

Gay/lesbian

The Wedding Banquet (1993). A gay New Yorker stages a marriage of convenience with a young woman to satisfy his traditional Taiwanese family, but the wedding becomes a major inconvenience when his parents fly in for the ceremony.

Personal Best (1982). Two women athletes participating in the 1980 Olympics fall in love during training.

Philadelphia (1994). A gay lawyer is unjustly fired by his firm because he has AIDS. Another lawyer reluctantly takes the gay man's case and learns to overcome his misconceptions about the disease, about those who contract it, and about gay people in general.

Desert Hearts (1985). This is a poignant story of a lesbian love affair, based on Jane Rule's 1964 novel *Desert of the Heart*.

The Times of Harvey Milk (1983). This documentary details the life and career of Harvey Milk, the first openly gay city supervisor to be elected in San Francisco.

By the time you have seen all of these movies, I hope you have begun to discover many more, especially ones that feature groups not included in this list. Learning about cultural difference can be both unending and enriching.

READ ABOUT DIFFERENT CULTURES

Bookstores and libraries are filled with books about cultural differences. From fiction writers such as Maya Angelou, Bebe Moore Campbell, Amy Tan, and Gabriel García Marquez to scholars such as Edward T. Hall and Geert Hofstede, a growing number of books provide intercultural insights.

Intercultural Press, in Yarmouth, Maine, is a good source of books with a cross-cultural theme. They can be found on the Web at *www.interculturalpress.com*. You can get on their catalog mailing list by calling 1-800-370-2665, e-mailing them at books@interculturalpress.com, or writing to them at PO Box 700, Yarmouth, ME 04096.

Some of my favorite intercultural books are:

A powerful story of two cultures, each putting forth their best and most heartfelt efforts

Fadiman, Anne. *A Spirit Catches You and You Fall Down: A Hmong Child, Her American Doctors, and the Collision of Two Cultures.* New York: Noonday Press, 1997.

The first history book that I couldn't put down

Takaki, Ronald A. *A Different Mirror: A History of Multicultural America.* Boston: Little, Brown and Company, 1993.

A fun read with regard to nonverbal communication

Axtell, Roger E. *Gesture: The DOs and TABOOs of Body Language Around the World.* New York: John Wiley & Sons, 1991.

Culturally specific insights

Condon, John C. *Good Neighbors: Communicating with the Mexicans* (second edition). Yarmouth, ME: Intercultural Press, 1997.

Condon, John C. *With Respect to the Japanese.* Yarmouth, ME: Intercultural Press, 1984.

Tannen, Deborah. *You Just Don't Understand: Women and Men in Conversation.* New York: Ballantine Books, 1990.

Oregon stories

Gamboa, Erasmo and Carolyn M. Buan, eds., *Nosotros: The Hispanic People of Oregon, Essays and Recollections.* Portland: Oregon Council for the Humanities, 1995.

Tamura, Linda. *The Hood River Issei: An Oral History of Japanese Settlers in Oregon's Hood River Valley.* Urbana: University of Illinois, 1993.

A societal perspective that will lead to action

Henderson, George. *Our Souls to Keep: Black/White Relations in America.* Yarmouth, ME: Intercultural Press, 1999.

Kivel, Paul. *Uprooting Racism.* Gabriola Island, BC: New Society Publishers, 1996.

McClintock, Karen. *Sexual Shame: An Urgent Call to Healing.* Minneapolis, MN: Fortress Press, 2001.

Summerfield, Ellen. *Survival Kit for Multicultural Living.* Yarmouth, ME: Intercultural Press, 1997.

For deeper insight into the mind and skill sets

Hall, Edward T. *The Silent Language.* New York: Doubleday, Random House, Inc., 1981.

Hall, Edward T. *The Dance of Life: The Other Dimension of Time.* New York: Doubleday, Random House, Inc., 1983.

Hofstede, Geert. *Cultures and Organizations: Software of the Mind.* London: McGraw-Hill, 1997.

Russo, Kurt, ed. *Finding the Middle Ground: Insights and Applications of the Value Orientations Method.* Yarmouth, ME: Intercultural Press, 2000.

Ting-Toomey, Stella. *Communicating Across Cultures*. New York: Guilford Press, 1999.

Ting-Toomey, Stella and John Etzell. *Managing Intercultural Conflicts Wisely*. Thousand Oaks, CA: Sage Publications, 2001.

Triandis, Harry, C. *Individualism and Collectivism*. Boulder, CO: Westview Press, 1995.

For insights into U.S. culture

Althen, Gary. *American Ways: A Guide for Foreigners in the United States*. Yarmouth, ME: Intercultural Press, 1988.

Kim, Eun Y. *The Yin and Yang of American Culture: A Paradox*. Yarmouth, ME: Intercultural Press, 2001.

Stewart, Edward C. and Milton J. Bennett. *American Cultural Patterns: A Cross-Cultural Perspective*. Yarmouth, ME: Intercultural Press, 1991.

And finally, if you want to leave home....

VISIT OTHER CULTURES!

Nothing beats spending time in other cultures after you have spent time preparing for the experience! There is value in living as the people from the culture live rather than as a tourist. Expect culture shock in the new culture, and give yourself time to adjust to reentry shock when you return home.

Chapter 13

TOWARD INCLUSIVE COMMUNITIES

After reading the previous 12 chapters, you might be feeling both excited about practicing the mind, heart, and skill sets and overwhelmed by the complexity of this information. My hope is that you will use your excitement to begin practicing new ways to include others.

Acknowledge your feeling of being overwhelmed. Then, let it go by focusing on one place you want to begin. Choose a context, such as home, work, or a community group, in which you can begin observing differences. You might want to choose one person with whom you can begin to practice. Start simply, but the key is to start!

INTEGRATING NEW KNOWLEDGE

I began this book by saying that working with difference is about our own cultural awareness of self and how we interact with others.

Sometimes a new awareness has a major impact on my current sense of self. When this happens, I am in an uncomfortable struggle between my comfortable, settled self and my emergent new self. When I am integrating new knowledge into who I am, I must take time to attend to myself.

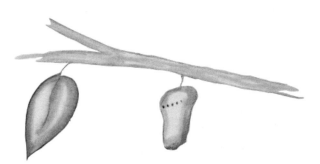

I can do this in several ways:

- Breathe deeply and remind myself that I am the best person I know how to be at this moment. In other words, my self before this new awareness was acting from my current "best."

- See that life is an unfolding journey of new discovery. To help me develop clarity about what this new awareness really means to me, I write about what I am experiencing—my thoughts and feelings.

- Give myself time to simply sit with this new awareness and not consciously come to any conclusion about what I will do with it.

- When ready, I begin to experiment with this new awareness as a means of incorporating the new idea or behavior into my everyday life.

In time, this new knowledge becomes a part of who I am and the continual learning cycle (described on pages 186–187) begins anew.

A LIFELONG PROCESS

Becoming aware of myself as a cultural person and how my culture manifests itself every day is an ongoing, lifelong process. I doubt that I ever will bring into consciousness all of who I am culturally. Thus, every day brings surprises.

Sometimes I like what I learn about myself. Sometimes I want to deny a part of myself. What I have found is that if I stay open to learning about myself, I become clearer about how I interact with others, especially those who are very different from me.

Practicing cultural self-awareness is like learning to rollerblade. It is wobbly and awkward at first. Sometimes I become paralyzed and wonder whether I can be natural with anyone again. However, with time and practice, focusing on cultural self-awareness becomes an easier part of all of my interactions.

PRACTICING THE SKILLS

When I am with another, I listen with attentiveness to what is being communicated so as to understand the other's meaning. When I know the other person is from a different culture, I listen and watch for styles—both verbal and nonverbal—and where they fit in the spectrum of possibilities.

I intentionally check for my own sense of resistance and become aware of my biases. I recognize that behavior that might seem "odd" or "different" to me might reflect cultural patterns common in the other person's experience.

I find it exciting to experience a style that is new to me and to see whether it fits within the communication style spectrum.

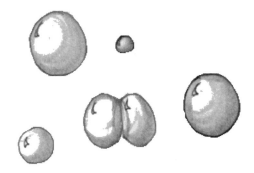

Sometimes I have ideas about what is being communicated, but I reserve judgment until I have checked it out with the other person. Sometimes the feedback increases my understanding, and sometimes I still am not sure what I am hearing.

I might need to spend time reflecting and, if possible, observing the person's interactions with others. I watch to learn what really is being communicated. In some ways, we are doing a communication dance, all the while staying open to learning.

Although we eventually can communicate a mutual understanding of meaning, I never will know what it is like to belong to another person's culture. I can only learn about the person's life experience through sharing, empathy, and listening.

I do believe we can work, live, and play together while maintaining our different cultures. We do not need to conform to each other in all that we do. The strength of culture lies in being with our own group. Each of us needs time to be where we are most comfortable and truly can "be" ourselves.

WORKING WITH COMPLEXITY

It is easy to have strong opinions and to impose our ideas and ways of acting on others. Sometimes we wish we could create order by telling everyone what to be and do, when to be and do it, and how to be and do it. We want the world to operate the "right" way, which is our way.

In this simple stage, only the people in my own group or culture feel respected, are heard, and have the opportunity to develop and share their gifts and talents. There is little awareness of the depth of diversity.

The person whose voice is not heard might shut down, both internally and externally. His or her potential to contribute to the community is lost. For the person in power (the one whose "right" way is heard and practiced), there might be a sense of frustration that not everyone willingly complies with the "right way." This person misses the richness of other perspectives.

Moving toward awareness of our own and others' cultures makes life more complex. It can be more confusing and uncertain as well. At the same time, there are more possibilities.

We can look back to times when life seemed simple and wonder how we can manage our more complex lives now. Learning to work with difference is similar. Life seemed simpler when my world worked only from one "right way," my way. As we become open to seeing others' ways of being, the idea of what is the "right way" expands from one to many.

Multiple perspectives add complexity. With practice, however, these multiple perspectives can become the expected way to view situations and problems. They can become a natural part of our daily interactions. When what we practice feels natural, it begins to seem simple rather than impossibly complex.

We can internalize a new way of communicating on a daily basis. The communication will be more situational, include more possibilities, and be more contextual, but it no longer will seem so complex. Instead, this fuzzy state of ambiguity will be seen as a normal part of communication. The intended result will be communities thriving from the inclusion of many more voices.

BUILDING COMMUNITY

When people are comfortable in their community, they might not realize why those who are culturally different do not join their community. When the community norms and climate support the culture of current members, the culturally different do not see how they could fit in. In fact, they may not even be aware of the possibility that they could be included in the community.

Whose responsibility is it to build inclusive communities? It is the responsibility of all of us.

Those who have the skills to include people who are different from mainstream community members are the ones who can initiate the building of an inclusive community.

The first steps are to identify a common goal to create a welcoming environment for all potential community members. From the perspective of the culturally different, what seems welcoming? To answer this question, community members must begin building relationships with people from differing cultures. The learning begins together, and the redesign of the community becomes mutual.

Building inclusive communities is a gradual process. With time, and an environment of mutual respect and sharing, the community will become more inclusive. It will continue to have tight, smaller in-groups, but in situations in which goals are shared mutually, the whole community will feel united.

IMAGING COMMUNITIES OF THE FUTURE

I can see communities of the future where everyone is included and has a meaningful role. Each person's voice is heard. Everyone cares about each member of the community. There is conflict, but people acknowledge it and try to work through it. When they can't come to a resolution, they give each other space until the time is ripe to try again. The resolution will be appropriate for the time, place, and context. It will not be for all time and all situations.

Everyone still will have their own distinctive cultures and will spend time with their own in-groups. They will respect those in their out-groups and interact with them as the need for community-building and getting work done arises.

The language about out-groups will change. It will be less judgmental and more positive. It will acknowledge that others do things differently, but the acknowledgment will not be a negative judgment.

This does not mean that we will never think or say negative things. It does mean that we will not stay in the negative thought space, because we are open to learning.

Even when we understand how others see the world, we might not want to see it that way ourselves. We still will know who we are and how we want to make meaning out of life. My way might be different from yours. There is space for both of our worldviews.

Through all of my interactions with others, I will know that...

The only person I can change is myself.

REFERENCES

Bennett, Milton J., ed. *Basic Concepts of Intercultural Communication: Selected Readings.* Yarmouth, ME: Intercultural Press, 1998.

Brewer, Marilynn B. and Norman Miller. *Intergroup Relations.* Pacific Grove, CA: Brooks/Cole, 1996.

Broom, Michael F., Ph.D., and Donald C. Klein, Ph.D. *Power: The Infinite Game.* Amherst, MA: HRD Press, 1995.

Cobbs, Price M. and William H. Grier. *The Jesus Bag.* New York: McGraw-Hill, 1971.

Deloria, Vine. *God Is Red: A Native View of Religion.* Golden, CO: Fulcrum Publishing, Inc., 1973.

Ferraro, Gary P. *The Cultural Dimension of International Business.* Englewood Cliffs, NJ: Prentice Hall, 1990.

Gerzon, Mark. *A House Divided: Six Belief Systems Struggling for America's Soul.* New York: Putnam, 1996.

Gilligan, Carol. *In a Different Voice: Pshchological Theory and Women's Development.* Cambridge, MA: Harvard University Press, 1993.

Grier, William and Price Cobbs. *Black Rage.* New York: Basic Books, Inc., 1968.

Gudykunst, William B., Stella Ting-Toomey, Sandra Sudweeks, and Lea P. Stewart. *Building Bridges: Interpersonal Skills for a Changing World.* Boston, MA: Houghton Mifflin Company, 1995.

Hall, Edward T. *Beyond Culture.* New York: Doubleday, Random House, Inc., 1976.

Hall, Edward T. *The Dance of Life: The Other Dimension of Time.* New York: Doubleday, Random House, Inc., 1983.

Hall, Edward T. *The Hidden Dimension.* New York: Doubleday, Random House, Inc., 1966.

Hall, Edward T. *The Silent Language.* New York: Doubleday, Random House, Inc., 1959.

Hofstede, Geert. *Cultures and Organizations: Software of the Mind.* London: McGraw-Hill, 1997.

Hofstede, Geert. *Culture's Consequences: Comparing Values, Behaviors, Institutions, and Organizations Across Nations* (second edition). Thousand Oaks, CA: Sage Publications, 2001.

Kluckhohn, Florence and Fred Strodtbeck. *Variations in Value Orientations.* Evanston, IL: Row, Peterson, 1961.

Knefelkamp, Lee. "An Overview of the Percy Scheme of Intercultural and Ethical Development." *Student Profile Readings.* Portland, OR: Intercultural Communication Institute, 1997. pp. 62–64.

Langer, Ellen J. *Mindfulness.* Reading, MA: Addison-Wesley Publishing Company, Inc., 1989.

Langer, Ellen J. *The Power of Mindful Learning.* Reading, MA: Addison-Wesley Publishing Company, Inc., 1997.

Loden, Marilyn and Judy B. Rosener. *Workforce America! Managing Employee Diversity as a Vital Resource.* Homewood, IL: Business One Irwin, 1991.

Markova, Dawna, Ph.D. *The Open Mind: Exploring the Six Patterns of Natural Intelligence.* Berkeley, CA: Conari Press, 1996.

Markus, Hazel and Shinobu Kitayama. "Culture and the Self: Implications for Cognition, Emotion, and Motivation." *Psychological Review* 2 (1991):224–253.

McCarthy, Bernice. *About Learning.* Barrington, IL: About Learning, Inc., 1996.

McGarty, Craig and S. Alexander Haslam, eds. *The Message of Social Psychology: Perspectives on Mind in Society.* Cambridge, MA: Blackwell, 1997.

McIntosh, Peggy. "White Privilege: Unpacking the Invisible Knapsack." *Peace and Freedom* (July/Aug 1989).

Myers, Isabel Briggs and Peter B. Myers. *Gifts Differing.* Palo Alto, CA: Consulting Psychologists Press, Inc., 1985.

Miller, Norman and Marilynn B. Brewer, eds. *Groups in Contact: The Psychology of Desegregation.* Orlando, FL: Academic Press, 1984.

Perry, William G. *Forms of Intellectual and Ethical Development in the College Years: A Scheme.* New York: Holt, Rinehart, and Winston, 1970.

Rodriguez, Luis J. *Always Running: La Vida Loca, Gang Days in L.A.* Willimantic, CT: Curbstone Press, 1993.

Russo, Kurt W., ed. *Finding the Middle Ground: Insights and Application of the Value Orientations Method.* Yarmouth, ME: Intercultural Press, 2000.

Samovar, Larry A. and Richard E. Porter. *Communication Between Cultures.* Belmont, CA: Wadsworth, 1995.

Satir, Virginia. *Making Contact.* Berkeley, CA: Celestial Arts, 1976.

Stephan, Walter G. and Cookie White Stephan. "Intergroup Anxiety." *Journal of Social Issues* 41 (1985):157–176.

Stephan, Walter G. and Cookie White Stephan. *Intergroup Relations.* Boulder, CO: Westview Press, 1996.

Summerfield, Ellen. *Crossing Cultures Through Film.* Yarmouth, ME: Intercultural Press, 1993.

Summerfield, Ellen and Sandra Lee. *Seeing the Big Picture: Exploring American Cultures on Film.* Yarmouth, ME: Intercultural Press, 2001.

Ting-Toomey, Stella. *Communicating Across Cultures.* New York: Guilford Press, 1999.

Triandis, Harry C. *Individualism and Collectivism.* Boulder, CO: Westview Press, 1995.